Unlocking School Bias

Unlocking
School Bias

Using Neuroscience to
Improve Student Outcomes

Horacio Sanchez

Foreword by David Flink

FOR INFORMATION:

Corwin

A SAGE Company

2455 Teller Road

Thousand Oaks, California 91320

(800) 233-9936

www.corwin.com

SAGE Publications Ltd.

1 Oliver's Yard

55 City Road

London EC1Y 1SP

United Kingdom

SAGE Publications India Pvt. Ltd.

Unit No 323-333, Third Floor, F-Block

International Trade Tower Nehru Place

New Delhi 110 019

India

SAGE Publications Asia-Pacific Pte. Ltd.

18 Cross Street #10-10/11/12

China Square Central

Singapore 048423

Vice President and
  Editorial Director: Monica Eckman

Publisher: Jessica Allan

Senior Content
  Development Editor: Mia Rodriguez

Project Editor: Amy Schroller

Copy Editor: Melinda Masson

Typesetter: C&M Digitals (P) Ltd.

Cover Designer: Rose Storey

Marketing Manager: Olivia Bartlett

Printed in the United States of America

Library of Congress Cataloging-in-Publication Data

Names: Sanchez, Horacio, author.

Title: Unlocking school bias : using neuroscience to improve student outcomes / Horacio Sanchez.

Description: Thousand Oaks, California : Corwin, [2025] | Includes bibliographical references and index.

Identifiers: LCCN 2024051621 | ISBN 9781071974001 (paperback) | ISBN 9781071974018 (epub) | ISBN 9781071974025 (epub) | ISBN 9781071974032 (pdf)

Subjects: LCSH: Discrimination in education. | Cognitive neuroscience. | Academic achievement. | Learning, Psychology of—Social aspects.

Classification: LCC LC212 .S26 2025 | DDC 370.8—dc23/eng/20241107
LC record available at https://lccn.loc.gov/2024051621

This book is printed on acid-free paper.

25 26 27 28 29 10 9 8 7 6 5 4 3 2 1

CONTENTS

FOREWORD

In 2014, in my book *Thinking Differently*, I wrote about being a neurodiverse third grader long before the term *neurodiverse* became more commonplace. My primary problem, as a third-grade student, was that I couldn't read at anywhere near grade-level standards and I acted impulsively, according to my teacher, Mrs. K, and our school principal. When my mother came to school to speak with Mrs. K about my troubling behavior, Mrs. K directed me to sit outside her classroom on the cold linoleum floor, where another "bad" student had drawn a frown face in a small pile of dust. Sitting there, feeling ashamed without really understanding why, I heard Mrs. K say to my mother, "He must try harder. Just encourage David to try."

What made her think that I hadn't been trying? I'd been trying, with all my might, every day since starting school. How had she put me in this lousy box?

Fast-forward to fifth grade. I found out that I was in fact dyslexic and had attention deficit hyperactivity disorder (ADHD). However, knowing all this didn't change everything immediately. My neurodiverse identity gave me something—accommodations and more kindness and understanding from my teachers—but I was still living in a world in which everyone, including me, constantly made assumptions about how people with dyslexia and ADHD thought, felt, and performed in school. I couldn't simply dodge these assumptions the way you might dodge a shark while swimming off the beaches in Florida.

And why?

Because biases were—and remain—the water, not the shark. As my brilliant friend Horacio Sanchez writes in the book you now hold in your hands, each of us has "automated biases [that] are always present, acting as lenses through which we see the world." This means we respond to situations and people according to how our subconscious mind perceives them. The scary thing is that our perceptions are often, very terribly, wrong.

I'm living proof of this. Although from a young age certain adults perceived me as someone who didn't or wouldn't try, I had within me as much drive, determination, and grit as my highest-achieving peers. With appropriate support for dyslexia and ADHD, I changed my trajectory in school. After high school, I attended Brown University and then Columbia for my master's degree. I became an educator, nonprofit leader, and author. These days I also teach at the Ivy League schools I attended.

At every step of my journey, I've become better at intentionally pushing against pervasive societal biases, specifically those allowing even the most well-meaning adults to think kids with learning disabilities don't try, can't learn, or won't ever achieve their potential. I've devoted my career to "fighting the water," addressing the biases that stunt student achievement and well-being.

And yet, I'm still learning and reflecting on this work every day, because, like everyone else in the world, I can't stop swimming in biases. I swim in biases when I teach, when I write, when I lead my staff at The Neurodiversity Alliance, when I take care of and make decisions concerning my two young children, and even when I think about who I am as an individual as well as a husband, son, and friend.

In this book, with Horacio as your guide, you'll discover the neuroscience behind implicit biases; how biases are formed and confirmed by the amygdala, the part of the brain triggering emotion and action, often within 200 milliseconds; how patterns in one's environment (home, classroom, workplace, and community) create biases and change how the brain develops; and, along with all this, simple actions you can take to counteract biases. Using the latest research, Horacio shows you why addressing implicit biases is a daily mindful practice. Human brains, he shows, are wired for automated actions. We must check ourselves, and check ourselves again, and again, every single day, to stop the subconscious mind from determining our thoughts and behavior.

Horacio and I became friends after meeting several times as speakers at conferences. Oddly enough, I was still surprised when he asked me to write the foreword to his book. I'm known for giving talks about neurodiversity—the word we now use for the idea that people experience and interact with the world in many different ways. I'd never heard Horacio use the word *neurodiversity* in his presentations. As soon as I began reading his book, however, I realized that his work fundamentally mirrors mine, and mine his. If you know and care about neurodiversity, you're no doubt aware that it's still a new concept, and that many people are just now learning about it, embracing the science behind it, and forming new perceptions about how kids—and adults—learn and achieve.

We have a long way to go, but together we can create a world in which the adverse outcomes associated with implicit bias are significantly reduced and even obliterated—a world that believes everyone can flourish, including neurodiverse learners who tend to think and solve problems differently. Whether you're an educator, a parent, a working professional, or another kind of leader, I hope this book will give you the research, tools, and inspiration you need to "swim" stronger and more intentionally in the rough waters we live in.

David Flink, Author, Founder, and
CEO of The Neurodiversity Alliance

ABOUT THE AUTHOR

 **Horacio Sanchez**, a national speaker and author, is an educational consultant to many organizations focused on improving formal education. He is recognized as one of the nation's leading authorities on resiliency and applied neuroscience. His expertise helps schools overcome the impact of poverty, improve school climate, engage in brain-based instruction, and address issues related to implicit bias. He is the author of the best-selling books *The Education Revolution* and *The Poverty Problem*.

Faith guides me; my wife inspires me.

INTRODUCTION

We all live with bias. It is impossible not to be biased because the brain is hardwired with certain biases from birth—it is programmed to be biased when encountering others. Then, our world will bias us further because disproportionate patterns in our environment also bias the brain. We can be biased by people, experiences, and repeated messages pervasive in the world around us. It is time to accept it: We all live life on the bias.

Bias has become a popular topic. Certain sound bites become prevalent whenever a topic becomes popular, and a false sense of understanding inevitably arises. Many of these views are erroneous and predictably lead to false narratives that do more harm than good. For example, years back, resiliency theory had become a popular topic, and suddenly, resiliency experts were as common as the Toyota Camry. There were two frequently heard messages: Every student needs one adult to care for them unconditionally to become resilient, and students who survive traumatic experiences show remarkable resilience because they possess the fortitude to carry on. Although people found to be resilient seem to have at least one long-term relationship with a caring adult, that fact alone does not make them resilient. They still need to acquire enough protective factors to counteract the risk in their lives. Also, surviving trauma speaks to our survival drive, not to our level of resilience. Resilient people achieve life success in the face of trauma and do not merely survive to experience bad life outcomes.

Once sound bites become prevalent, people repeat them with the confidence of a PhD candidate defending their dissertation. Sound bites can become so pervasive that they seep into every aspect of our society, being reiterated in social media, print media, television, movies, and even songs. These repeated messages can unwittingly bias us further because they tend to be subconsciously accepted as truth even if they oppose our value system. How many times have you heard that Asians are good at science and math and never stopped to examine the statement?

The truth is that implicit bias occurs subconsciously and at a rate of speed so fast that the conscious brain is unaware that it happened. Therefore, implicit biases influence our thoughts and actions before they are formulated. As a result, most of us walk around acknowledging the outcomes of bias but completely unaware when we are complicit. Since we are unaware of our implicit biases, the lack of motivation to address them is logical. Who runs out to put out a fire that no one sees burning?

The road to addressing implicit bias has two divergent paths. One is blind faith, where we confess that we have committed biased acts but we don't know when or why. The other, the road less traveled, is based on neuroscience, which helps us understand how our brains produce bias, predict when it is probable, and engage in appropriate responses.

This book is written to end the confusion around bias and to provide educators with research and strategies that will enable them to address the issues of bias without guilt and accusations. Neuroscience allows us to understand that we all are biased. Implicit bias first occurred before we could formulate independent thought. We all possess a higher number of implicit biases than we could ever estimate, and not all of them are necessarily bad. Positive biases can provide a better disposition, help our social interactions, and even improve our physiology. To those who use the knowledge of implicit bias to assail others, I say, let him who is without bias cast the first stone.

CHAPTER 1

·····································

THE BIRTH OF BIAS

A Love Story

▶ In-group bias is an unintended outcome of infant–mother attachment. The bonding hormone **oxytocin** plays a role in in-group cooperation, resulting in diminished collaboration with out-group members. In-group bias begins before a child can formulate independent thought or exercise choice.

A BABY'S LIFE: THE FIRST 12 MONTHS

Imagine being in a comfy womb, taking as many naps as you want. Your loyal butler, Placenta, delivers your meals around the clock. Then, suddenly, your home is raided, and you are unceremoniously dragged out of your pampered existence into the real world. No wonder Otto Rank described the birth experience as a traumatic, violent, physical, and psychic separation from your mother (Rank, 1929). The British psychoanalyst Wilfred Bion wrote that children are born into an inner state of chaos and confusion because whatever they feel is unknown and undistinguishable (Bion, 1977). Bion also posited that a baby is born before rational thinking comes into being, making the experience unfathomable. Thank God we no longer welcome a baby into the world by holding them upside down and slapping their backside. Birth is traumatic enough.

In truth, what a baby is feeling at birth are just conjectures. None of us can recall the birth experience or the first years of life. However, neuroscience does provide a few salient points of clarification that are reliable. Humans struggle with change. Change alerts the amygdala's fight-or-flight response, spiking cortisol and causing an increase in your heart rate and blood pressure. At the very least, change challenges our homeostasis—our equilibrium. Now imagine change from an infant's point of view. The brain achieves comprehension of new experiences by being able to associate them with prior life events. Babies have nothing to which to compare the initial changes they experience. That makes new information more chemically charged than things with which we are familiar. When we are unable to connect new information to something we already know, the brain undergoes a chemical upheaval, creating a sense of unease. The amygdala is always alerted to new experiences because it must make sure you are not in danger. As a result, a child's temperament is put to the test within the first minute of life. Infants with difficult or shy and anxious temperaments have a dramatic physiological response to the experiences of birth, which is why they are likely to perceive it as a traumatic event. Studies show that the early experiences and environmental influences of infants with more fragile temperaments can leave a lasting signature on their genetic predispositions that can affect the emerging brain's architecture for their lifespan (Shonkoff et al., 2012).

> *The early experiences and environmental influences of infants with more fragile temperaments can leave a lasting signature on their genetic predispositions.*

0–6 Months

An infant's earliest form of communication is, at its core, a display of emotion. If their needs are not understood and quickly met, they experience frustration, and an increased emotional outburst is manifested. The state of utter dependency for some infants is exhausting and can lead to a persistent state of anxiety. The human infant begins life more helplessly than any other living creature. Imagine being an infant with an unresponsive caretaker. Your needs are not met, your cries increase until you are physically spent, and your body shuts down from sheer exhaustion. It is easy to understand why the quality of care and environment in the early days of life can have lifelong ramifications.

Empathy

At the same time, infants are born with a superpower that helps them survive until they can communicate with words—the ability to understand and produce emotional expression. The capacity to understand the emotions of others is the foundation of **empathy**. Empathy is the process the brain utilizes to not only identify the emotions of others but also feel what the other person is experiencing. The brain goes through a three-step process in producing empathy. First, mirror neurons activate; this step triggers motor neurons in the brain to engage as if we are doing the emotion we are witnessing (Rizzolatti & Craighero, 2004). Next, the **amygdala**, the part of the brain intricately involved in producing emotions, assigns a chemical signature to the experience, which enables us to feel what the other person is feeling at a biological level (Carr et al., 2003). Then, the **insula** interfaces between the mirror neuron system and the amygdala to bring social-emotional context to what is being observed (Dapretto et al., 2006). The importance of emotional comprehension cannot be understated; it is essential for effective human interaction.

Infants are born with an innate capacity to express basic emotions and have an intuitive knowledge of the meaning of the major emotional expressions displayed by others (Ekman, 2003). Many early researchers limited this ability to reading only facial expressions, but babies seem to intuit emotion in voice tone, hand gestures, and body posture. Parents are often surprised to see how alert a newborn is. Immediately after birth, a newborn's eyes are open, and they spend a lot of time studying faces. Babies react to the sound of others' voices and utilize all their senses, including smell and touch, to further identify and bond with their caregivers. The ability to quickly recognize, label, and display basic emotions draws adults to the infant and keeps them engaged. Think about the amount of time an adult is willing to spend with an infant who repeatedly smiles in response to a game of peekaboo. Now imagine how many adults are not willing or able to engage with the infant. The infant may begin to mimic the blank stare of the adult who lacks emotional expressions. It is essential that we comprehend just how important understanding emotional expression is to human experience. Empathy is right up there with feeding and social bonding as essential to survival. The ability to express and read emotions begins to be cultivated from the first day of life.

> *The ability to express and read emotions begins to be cultivated from the first day of life.*

The repeated labeling of emotions during social interactions leads to the aptitude to anticipate what emotion will happen next. A baby begins to learn that their smile can trigger a smile in another person. In this moment, the unpredictable world becomes more predictable. Most of these social interactions are transpiring with the primary caregivers, leading to the association of safety and nurturance being identified with parents. Babies gain a mental script of daily interactions that form the basic building blocks of attachment with their caregivers.

One of the functions of **mirror neurons** is to teach social behavior that happens at a predictable time and in a predictable setting (Jeon & Lee, 2018). Therefore, a baby becomes hyper-focused on the expressions of the caregiver and learns what responses make them happy or sad. The intensity of focus on emotional expressions causes an imprinting of the face or faces associated with safety and security. The result is that the emotions of the caregivers have a greater neurobiological impact. When the caregiver is sad, the infant is sad; when the caregiver is happy, the infant is happy. The foundations of positive social interactions are being laid. A look of approval by the caregiver triggers mirror neurons, activating motor neurons in the infant's brain that mimic their expressions, and the amygdala, assigning a positive chemical signature that the baby feels. Positive looks provide a wonderful feeling that is rewarding and sought by the infant. Looks of disapproval, on the other hand, provide a negative chemical experience that the baby seeks to avoid. Belsky and colleagues went as far as to suggest that insecure infants are biased toward the recollection of negative memories, while secure infants are biased toward the recollection of positive memories (Belsky et al., 1996). One of life's most profound lessons is taught very early in life: The attitude you project influences the responses you receive.

> *Insecure infants are biased toward the recollection of negative memories, while secure infants are biased toward the recollection of positive memories (Belsky et al., 1996).*

The predictable positive exchange of expressions sets in motion healthy prosocial behaviors. Research has found that the foundation of attachment is predictive of age-appropriate emotional recognition later in childhood (Steele et al., 2008). It is not surprising that children who do not develop a positive attachment with caregivers often suffer from poor social behavior, which might be rooted in poor emotional cognition. Research indicates that by the sixth month of life, infants have already been exposed to 32,000 highly articulated contingent facial expressions of emotion (Malatesta, 1985). No wonder the infant and caregiver can reach such an elevated level of empathy that they can experience periods of brain-to-brain synchronization. **Brain-to-brain synchronization** occurs when the brain waves of two individuals synchronize in brain regions simultaneously, creating an emotional resonance, further strengthening the social bonds, and motivating prosocial behavior within the pair (Peng et al., 2021).

> *Children who do not develop a positive attachment with caregivers often suffer from poor social behavior, which might be rooted in poor emotional cognition.*

It is persistent interactions with a significant other who is consistently available and supportive in times of distress and stress that facilitate the sense of attachment and give rise to a sense of self. Having a **secure attachment** sets a trajectory for future physiology. The theory is that a secure attachment lowers anxiety and avoidance, and the individual therefore reacts to stressful events with lower levels of distress and physiological arousal (Feeney & Kirkpatrick, 1996; Mikulincer & Florian, 1998). Also, a secure attachment provides a child with a more positive expectation about people and relationships, improving the likelihood that people with similar outlooks will be drawn to the child (Collins, 1996; Collins & Read, 1990). It is important to recognize that an attraction toward positive people is established early in life. Although children with a secure attachment to a primary caretaker often demonstrate a more favorable reaction toward novel stimuli and interactions with strangers, resilience seems to have some limits (Arend et al., 1979; Moss et al., 1997).

> *A secure attachment lowers anxiety and avoidance, and the individual therefore reacts to stressful events with lower levels of distress and physiological arousal (Feeney & Kirkpatrick, 1996; Mikulincer & Florian, 1998).*

6–12 Months

In-Group Bias

The dark side of attachment is the activation of fear. Initially, infants with a secure attachment still demonstrate a fear of strangers (Bronson, 1968; Collard, 1967). Most individuals exposed to infants have witnessed that they are frightened by strangers, and unfamiliar objects and places can alert them to danger. In unfamiliar situations, the infant experiences feelings of anxiety and seeks out proximity to attachment figures to feel supported and safe. The infant begins to categorize people into familiar and unfamiliar groupings. The familiar is associated with a positive physiological response, and the unfamiliar is associated with a negative physiological response. Over time, the safe category is expanded to siblings, extended family, and close family friends. The safe group over time is defined as "us" (the in-group), and the unfamiliar as "them" (the out-group) (Allport, 1954). This is not merely a cognitive process but an emotional one rooted in involuntary physiological responses.

> **The dark side of attachment is the activation of fear.**

Every day, relying on primary caretakers for survival links survival with the caregivers and, eventually, people who look like the caregivers. Being drawn to gaze and noticing your primary caregiver's emotions and being impacted makes looking at and reading **in-group** members attractive. Aversion to strangers lowers the desire and the ease of noticing and reading the emotional cues of **out-group** members. The calming physiological response is felt when in the presence of your primary caregiver and eventually around extended family and friends. The feeling of safety with the in-group is not felt when in the presence of strangers and, eventually, people in the "other" category. Everything signals loudly that "I am safe with my parents, family, and friends—us." It is love and nurturance that have formed an in-group bias. Every day, an in-group presence exists without consistent positive exposure to out-group members, which further solidifies the reaction of the mind and body. Studies show that by 3 to 9 months of age, infants already are demonstrating an in-group bias and reacting favorably to the faces of members of their own group and less so toward those of other races (Sangrigoli & De Schonen, 2004; Xiao, Quinn et al., 2018; Xiao, Wu et al., 2018). **In-group preference** seems consistent across differing races, genders, and ages (Langlois et al., 1991).

> **By 3 to 9 months of age, infants already are demonstrating an in-group bias and reacting favorably to the faces of members of their own group and less so toward those of other races (Sangrigoli & De Schonen, 2004; Xiao, Quinn et al., 2018; Xiao, Wu et al., 2018).**

It is important to note the subtle nature of **implicit bias**. An infant's in-group preference is formulated before choice or conscious awareness has been developed. Babies do not have conscious awareness that bias influences their thoughts and actions. Implicit bias occurs at 150 to 200 milliseconds (100% subconscious), while conscious thought does not occur until around 600 milliseconds. This allows infants' thoughts and actions to not only seem logical but, more importantly, feel normal. It is the breaking of the patterns of in-group preference that will cause adverse reactions in the mind and body.

> *An infant's in-group preference is formulated before choice or conscious awareness has been developed.*

Consider the influences that in-group preference born of love will produce. It will influence attractions, initial friendships, and eventually partner selection, reinforcing the preference. The amygdala, the emotional brain, is already drawn to things that are familiar. As a result, an in-group exposure does not cause an adverse reaction, while an out-group presence will alert the amygdala. Furthermore, in-group preference promotes cooperation with the thoughts and actions of in-group members. The cooperation associated with in-group preference is connected to the oxytocin attachment between infant and primary caregiver (often the parent). Research shows that in-group cooperation is conditioned by oxytocin and is intuitive rather than deliberate (Ten Velden et al., 2017). The opposite of cooperation is disagreement. Oxytocin does not promote disagreement; rather, by increasing a natural desire to agree with in-group members, it creates a natural tendency to disagree with opposing viewpoints. Repeated agreements with in-group members over time create a point of view or a way of thinking. Once established, patterns are hard for the brain to change because they are reinforced with dopamine (Wickens et al., 2007). It is the surge of dopamine in the **nucleus accumbens** that makes **habits**.

> *In-group cooperation is conditioned by oxytocin and is intuitive rather than deliberate (Ten Velden et al., 2017).*

It is safe to say that by the end of the first year of life, two things have already been established. A bond between the infant and the primary caretaker is forged by oxytocin. Also, an in-group preference is established and reinforced by oxytocin and dopamine. The conductor of Implicit Bias Railways has just yelled, "All aboard," and the train is not only on the track; it has already hit such high speeds that applying the brakes will only slow its progress but not bring the train to a stop.

RECOMMENDATIONS FOR EDUCATORS

1. Encourage Variance and Exposure

What it is: It is a safe assumption that most parents are not intentionally attempting to program an in-group preference. On the contrary, most parents would be appalled at the notion that parental attachment gave birth to such a reaction toward certain people. However, studies have found that several conditions can mitigate in-group bias on the part of infants. Having interracial parents has been shown to influence in-group preference (Bar-Haim et al., 2006). Children being exposed to parents who look different from each other makes researchers wonder if other forms of early exposure could reduce in-group bias. Socially diverse environments that provide a greater range of exposure to people of different races also seem to influence the preferences of infants. For example, infants with early and consistent exposure to different races do not show a preference for their own race at 3 months of age (Bar-Haim et al., 2006).

The research findings suggest that exposure to in-group versus out-group faces can lower in-group preference and improve the recognition of the physical characteristics of out-group members (K. Lee et al., 2017). Training at the preschool level to recognize out-group faces has reduced implicit racial bias. Teachers can implement this training through a variety of simple activities. For instance, students can be asked to look at pictures of out-group members and associate each picture with a child's name. Then, later, they can see how many students can remember the correct name corresponding to the picture. Another effective activity is to read stories with pictures of out-group characters and review the stories to see if students can recognize and name the characters (Heron-Delaney et al., 2011). These simple activities serve two purposes: to promote recognition of people with different features and to humanize them by encouraging students to remember their names.

What it looks like in practice:

- Imagined Play

Imagined play with out-group members consistently reduces intergroup bias among children (Cameron et al., 2006). Some visuals are useful to help students. Figurines representing different groups or faces of students from different groups glued to Popsicle sticks work well (actual faces of children work better than cartoon faces because the brain reacts differently to pictures of actual people than it does to a cartoon representation). Then, different scenarios are created for students to do during imagined play.

- Empathy Scenario

Students are instructed to help their new friend, who fell on the playground, by checking if he is okay. This scenario incorporates the key elements of empathy, identification of emotions, and response. Teachers can elevate the effectiveness of this exercise by having students imagine how the new student's face will look after he has fallen and how it will change after they have helped him.

- Social Skills Scenario

Students practice two elements of social skills identified by neuroscience to build rapport. They are instructed to imagine that the figurine representing them is meeting a new out-group student. The students are instructed to imagine smiling while approaching the new student, introducing themselves by saying hi and their name. Then, they are instructed to ask the new student what her name is. Students are instructed to ask the new student what she likes to do for fun, and find something they both like.

Neuroscience has identified two key elements of social skills: disarming the amygdala with a smile, which lowers the amygdala activation to differences, and triggering amygdala attraction by focusing on what two people have in common. Research shows that the amygdala becomes attracted when we identify a commonality (Adolphs, 2010).

- Cooperation Scenario

Cooperation is a natural outcome of empathy; when cooperation is emphasized, empathy is enhanced. In cooperation scenarios, the students imagine themselves working with an out-group member to achieve a goal that cannot be completed unless they work together. For example, both must get on the other side of a wall too high to get over on their own.

Why it works:

Three types of childhood experiences were found to reduce intergroup bias reliably (Skinner & Meltzoff, 2019):

- *Structured intergroup play on a consistent basis.* Intergroup playdates must be a conscious decision and may require effort. Making a conscious decision to ensure that a child has consistent social exposure to out-group members is an investment in the child developing a higher level of comfort with the people they will deal with in a diverse world.

The most effective way to achieve diverse groupings is to engage in activities in which students discover things they have in common with other students. The teacher can then group students by things they have in common, carefully creating diverse student groups. It is recommended that students engage in an activity that requires them to work together to achieve a required goal physically. Embodied cognition determines that the brain anchors abstract concepts to concrete things to improve our understanding. An activity in which you physically cooperate with others will quickly anchor the concept of cooperation with out-group members. Many team-building activities work well. One example is the life raft activity. Groups of four to six students must stand on a 2-foot-diameter circle for 60 seconds without any part of their bodies touching the ground outside the circle. Each student group will engage in problem-solving, planning, and figuring out how to physically support one other so that everyone can fit in the circle for 60 seconds. When they are ready, they call the teacher to check if everyone is in the circle and to count down the 60 seconds. Successfully achieving the task instantly bonds the group based on a sense of accomplishment and dependency on one another.

- *Imagined play with out-group members.* Imagined play with out-group members usually requires access to toys and books that reflect diversity. When children have consistent exposure to diversity in toys and books, it enables their imaginations to create diverse friends during imagined play.

Teachers should consider creating imaginary play scenarios and finding books emphasizing empathy and cooperation. Empathy will enable students to put themselves in the out-group member's place. It has also been found to promote cooperation. By emphasizing cooperation with an out-group member, empathy is increased.

- *Correction and redirection when exposed to prejudiced behaviors or ideas.* One of the ways the amygdala establishes values during childhood is based on correction by parents when the child engages in inappropriate behaviors. When caregivers redirect, the child observes something not in line with family values. Parents who share their values on how all people should be treated consistently produce children with similar values. Parents who voice their disapproval of the unfair treatment of people based on race, religion, gender, or disability establish early family values that are protected by the amygdala.

Teachers should always be sensitive to behaviors or comments that promote prejudice and gently correct and redirect behaviors. For example, a student might tell his friend that Juan talks funny. The teacher might hear the comment and, rather than ignoring it, take the time to help the student understand that Juan is from a different country and speaks two languages. If he were a student in Juan's country, he would speak differently from the students there. Would he like that the students might think he sounds strange because he is from another country that speaks a different language?

CONCLUSION

Our values begin in our emotional brain and are based on our experiences. The brain protects established values by allowing the amygdala to filter incoming information before it reaches the **cortex**, the part of the brain responsible for rational decision-making. When new information contradicts established values, the amygdala attempts to bias our opinion toward the information to increase the probability that it will be rejected.

CHAPTER 2

....

THE CUP IS
HALF EMPTY

Negative Bias

CHAPTER OVERVIEW

▶ Having a negative bias means having a tendency to weigh negative information, events, or emotions more strongly than neutral or even positive stimuli (Baumeister et al., 2001; Rozin & Royzman, 2001). In fact, negative stimuli can have a stronger impact on almost every aspect of our lives than positive information and impacts our attention, perception, memory, physiology, affect, behavior, motivation, and decision-making. Baumeister's extensive study concluded that a negativity bias in humans is so reliable that it can be considered a fundamental principle of human behavior (Baumeister et al., 2001). This is not to say that humans are doomed to always focus on the bad or that misery will prevail as our default disposition. However, it seems that for positive information to prevail over negative stimuli, a superior number of "good" events must transpire. The reality is that when good and bad are present in equal numbers, the bad will overwhelm the good. Therefore, people must be intentional in attending to the good to achieve healthy brain function.

NEGATIVE BIAS

Have you ever been creeping along a highway due to a terrible accident, only to find out that a lane was open, but drivers passed the accident at 5 miles per hour to get a more extended look? This is more than a morbid curiosity: Humans' attention is drawn toward the negative. The tendency is so strong that we are alerted to negative things in our environment faster than positive. In fact, the function is so automated that when we read, our eyes focus on negative emotional words faster and longer than positive words (Scott et al., 2012). Our predisposition to attend to the negative is part of our **preattentional system,** which refers to a cognitive process that mediates the selection of the most important information in the environment (Wolfe & Utochkin, 2019). In other words, before your conscious mind has a chance to select what you should focus on, your subconscious mind directs your attention toward negative things in the environment.

> *We are alerted to negative things in our environment faster than positive.*

It is thought that the preattentional system evolved because humans consistently focused on certain things with such regularity that the brain developed an automated process to ensure that selected things would be observed. The process is so efficient that it occurs in milliseconds, and our conscious mind is often unaware of the observation. What the subconscious mind observes will bias conscious thoughts and actions. In many ways, the preattentional system best explains implicit bias. Much of the time, we are biased; we may be blissfully unaware, but something we briefly saw or heard has influenced us.

Memory

Negative bias constantly alters our perceptions of the world without us being aware. No place is the impact more evident than with memory. Negative bias influences what we learn and remember as well as the intensity of those memories. The subconscious mind brings back past learning and experiences to help us make better decisions in the present. Some of the information we consciously weigh, but a lot of the information influencing our decisions comes from subconscious memories. The logic is simple: If our brain is prone to remembering negative information more frequently, then negative memories are constantly biasing our everyday thoughts and actions.

Consider that parents constantly teach their children words and are usually focused on positive vocabulary. Despite these efforts to instill a positive vocabulary, by age 3, the number of positive words remains the same, but the number of negative words doubles (Lagattuta & Wellman, 2002). Spend time with a happy, healthy 3-year-old, and one quickly notices that her favorite word is *no*. She even says no when what she wants to say is yes. Want to go to the park? No. Ride your new bike? No. But you love the park, and your cousin will be there. No. Fifteen minutes later, she is excitedly skipping to the park. Not only do children remember negative words faster, but all negative information is also learned faster and will last longer (Dreben et al., 1979). Have a parent say a bad word in the vicinity of their distracted child. Suddenly, the child's ears perk up, and you hear an elongated "Ooh, Daddy said a bad word." Researchers have found that people remember unpleasant memories longer. In addition, studies have found that negative events leave a longer and more lasting mark on memory (Banaji & Hardin, 1994). Some memories can negatively alter our affect and physiology, increasing stress, breathing, and heart rate. It is not surprising that traumatic events often bring back vivid memories that alter cognitive and physical function. Some traumatized individuals struggle to suppress traumatic memories from intruding at inopportune times, reducing their ability to function at a productive level.

> *Some memories can negatively alter our affect and physiology, increasing stress, breathing, and heart rate.*

Children will grow up remembering bad behavior better than good conduct (Skowronski & Carlston, 1987). Negative bias condemns us to a lifetime of reliving embarrassing moments and unbecoming behaviors shared by siblings. Remember when you thought you were so cool and tried smoking in the bathroom? You heard someone coming and panicked, throwing the cigarette out and running, only to find out you set the trash can on fire. However, even negative bias has its limitations. Although we are better at remembering the negative behaviors of others, we are not as good at recalling our own bad conduct (Skowronski et al., 1991). Not only do we remember negative behaviors, but we also tend to remember the bad traits others possess while minimizing their good ones (Pratto & John, 1991).

> *Although we are better at remembering the negative behaviors of others, we are not as good at recalling our own bad conduct (Skowronski et al., 1991).*

Brain Response

Studies on negative bias have identified three main brain areas activated by negative stimuli: the right inferior frontal cortex, the insular cortex, and the amygdala. The right inferior frontal cortex and the insular cortex are involved in valence-based evaluations (Cunningham et al., 2004). The **valence-based approach** studies how emotions influence our judgments and choices. The involvement of these two brain regions should not be surprising because they play a role in evaluating implicit and explicit attraction and aversion stimuli. Whenever we experience a positive or negative response to something in our environment, the right inferior frontal cortex and insular cortex are activated. The amygdala is very involved in processing the more intense emotional responses to things we encounter. Therefore, these areas of the brain responding to negative bias make sense since negative stimuli are generally rated as emotionally more intense than neutral and positive experiences (Ito et al., 1998). Hertenstein and Campos found that 11-month-olds in positive conditions behaved much like 11-month-olds. However, 11-month-olds experiencing negative conditions did not display age-appropriate behavior and took some time to regain emotional and physical balance after being removed from the environment (Hertenstein & Campos, 2004). There seems to be a predictable encoding of the negative experiences at the neural level. After all, negative bias plays a role in our survival. An infant touches a hot stove, and the negative information is encoded so that months later, when approaching the stove, the negative memory impacts the child emotionally and physically, reducing the chances that the same behaviors occur again.

The Infant's Innate Negative Bias

If humans have evolved to possess a negative bias, it should be apparent during infancy. It has been well established that the emotional displays of mothers impact infants. In a classic study, Hornik had mothers use facial, vocal, or gesture expressions in response to a toy to see the impact it would have on infant behavior. While the infant responses to positive and neutral expressions varied, the reaction to a negative demonstration consistently produced toy avoidance

(Hornik et al., 1987). In a follow-up study, researchers found that a negative tone of voice in response to a toy caused infants not only to stop their approach toward a toy but also to increase their distance from the toy (Mumme et al., 1996; Sorce et al., 1985; Vaish & Striano, 2004).

Neuroscience research on infants' negative bias further validated these early behavioral response studies. Researchers studied infant brain response to a caregiver's emotions in novel situations. The results found that negative emotional expression by caregivers produced greater brain activation than positive or neutral responses (Carver & Vaccaro, 2007). The caregiver's responses influenced the infant's behavior toward objects in the environment and how the infant interacted with the caregiver. Negative stimuli produced an immediate and longer response in the brain. Similar studies found that a baby's attention toward negative stimuli occurs between 400 and 800 milliseconds after the onset of the stimuli (Courchesne et al., 1981; Nelson, 1994). The results show that a baby's attentional system quickly picks up any negative stimuli within the environment while not as quickly noticing neutral and positive objects or emotions. As the child gets older, the ability to attend to negative things in the environment will only increase in speed, making adverse observations occur within 200 milliseconds, resulting in the process becoming subconscious. These studies indicate a more immediate and greater impact of negative cues versus positive cues, suggesting that negativity bias is already present in the first year of life.

> *Negativity bias is already present in the first year of life.*

Biological Sex Differences

Because negative bias begins at birth, it is not surprising that it impacts all phases of our development. Males tend to have a slightly lower negativity bias than females (Norris, 2019).

A measure of prenatal testosterone exposure predicted the biological sex difference related to negativity bias (Manning et al., 1998; McIntyre, 2006). A smaller negativity bias is correlated with how testosterone increases risk-taking behaviors (Sapienza et al., 2009). When you engage in more risk-taking behavior, the brain is forced to mitigate some negative bias. Therefore, males with high levels of testosterone are more capable of impulsively engaging in high-risk behavior before being able to ascertain risk fully. In cases of engaging in high-risk behavior, males experience two emotional responses that occur before rational thoughts are formulated. In these cases, the chemical reward from risk-taking is stronger than the brain's weighing of possible negative outcomes.

Adolescents

The ability to make good decisions is based on the stabilization and development of the prefrontal cortex. Adolescents are more susceptible to negative bias compared to adults because the prefrontal cortex is not fully developed (Yuan et al., 2015). An immature prefrontal cortex exercises lower control over the amygdala, increasing the occurrence of impulsive behaviors. A study that compared the brain responses of adults to adolescents found enhanced brain susceptibility to emotionally negative stimuli in adolescents compared to adults (Yuan et al., 2015).

> *Adolescents are more susceptible to negative bias compared to adults because the prefrontal cortex is not fully developed (Yuan et al., 2015).*

Older Adult Differences

There is also a "positivity effect" in older adults. As we age, the chemical responses to emotions lower a little. The lowering of an emotional response seems to impact the functioning of a negativity bias, producing what is commonly called the positivity effect in older adults (Carstensen & DeLiema, 2018; Carstensen & Mikels, 2005). Older individuals experience a lowering of the intensity of negative emotions, and this tendency reduces their attention and memory toward negative information. In fact, a study found that older adults exhibit memory distortions for positive information in literature, movies, and images (Mather & Carstensen, 2005). However, this is not the absence of negative bias; it is the reduction of the intensity of the emotional response to negative stimuli.

Foundational Studies

Several comprehensive research reviews have established negativity bias beginning in infancy and continuing throughout adulthood (e.g., Baumeister et al., 2001; Rozin & Royzman, 2001; Taylor, 1991). The classic study that brought negative bias into the public stream of consciousness was conducted by Cacioppo. He conducted an **event-related potentials (ERPs)** study using pleasant and unpleasant images. An ERPs approach uses electroencephalography to capture neural activity related to both sensory and cognitive processes simultaneously. The study found that negative images elicited greater brain activation than neutral and even positive images (Cacioppo et al., 1999). What made this finding so profound was how much more significantly negative images impacted the brain compared to positive images.

However, these studies fail to bring to life the negative bias's impact on everyday life. How many of us have made a presentation to our peers only to have one evaluation out of a hundred ruin the feeling of a job well done? The dreaded annual personnel evaluation has us conditioned to ignore the 45 minutes of glowing reviews. At the same time, our ears are alerted to constructive criticism, becoming instantly despondent upon hearing one negative comment. One interesting illustration of negative bias involves Larry David, the co-creator of *Seinfeld*. He attended a Yankees game and saw his name and picture on the jumbotron. The announcer said, "In attendance tonight, Larry David, the co-creator of the *Seinfeld* show." Forty-six thousand fans stood to their feet and gave him a 5-minute standing ovation. Later that evening, while leaving the stadium, one fan yelled out, "Larry David, you suck" (Hiatt, 2011). At a social event held later that evening, friends of Larry said he was so upset that all he could talk about was the fan who insulted him. This story puts negative bias into clear perspective; one person's negative comment extinguished the glowing reviews of 46,000 adoring fans.

Relationships

Interpersonal relationships are one area in which negative bias most impacts us. When we meet someone, we will likely emphasize negative impressions more than positive ones in formulating an initial opinion (Abelson & Kanouse, 1966; Fiske & Taylor, 1991; Kanouse & Hanson, 1972; Skowronski & Carlston, 1987). Meeting someone and instantaneously liking them will occur less frequently than being neutral or disliking someone. The most common exception is when encountering someone with whom we share a lot in common. The reason for this is simple: The amygdala, which plays a significant role in the formulation of first impressions, is attracted to itself. We have evolved to have a more significant attraction to people like us.

> *When we meet someone, we will likely emphasize negative impressions more than positive ones in formulating an initial opinion (Abelson & Kanouse, 1966; Fiske & Taylor, 1991; Kanouse & Hanson, 1972; Skowronski & Carlston, 1987).*

Negative bias will continue to dictate the quality of our relationships for the rest of our lives. A married couple has two blissful weeks on vacation and thinks they cannot be happier.

And yet having one disagreement results in the contemplation of divorce. A longitudinal study found that couples who had initially shown higher rates of negative affect toward one another in the initial year of marriage reported greater declines in relationship satisfaction over the following 3 years. However, couples who demonstrated positive affect had no such decline in their relationship (Levenson & Gottman, 1985). In other words, a disapproving look is so pronounced that it can often damage the relationship. A similar conclusion emerged from a longitudinal study by Huston and colleagues. By following couples for more than a decade, they were able to ascertain that negativity early in a marital relationship was predictive of divorce 10 years later (Huston et al., 2001).

A lifelong friendship abruptly ends, rendering 20 years of shared appreciation for one another to be discarded due to one bitter argument. Negative bias is so predictable that it is safe to say that almost everyone knows of family members who no longer talk to each other over some slight that, if rationally evaluated, would be perceived by most individuals as trivial. It produces such strong emotions that it can cause rational, logical adults to walk away from valuable relationships over one negative conversation, action, or event.

Negative bias diminishes rational thought, promotes rash decisions, encourages gossip, and influences others to share their bad opinions. Although negative bias does serve a survival function, it is crucial that we are vigilant not to let it become extreme. We should actively attempt to see people's good qualities and truly evaluate how significant any event that jeopardizes relationships is in the larger scheme of things.

> *Negative bias diminishes rational thought, promotes rash decisions, encourages gossip, and influences others to share their bad opinions.*

Change

Another area where negative bias influences education is the ability to implement change. Why is change so hard for the human brain? Imagine being a teacher in a district where you are being trained in new reading strategies that will replace the program you have utilized for 5 years. Since the old reading strategies have been used consistently for 5 years, they have reached a level of automation that requires very low energy from the brain. Low brain energy results in lower cognitive effort and an increased ability to attend to other related tasks. Effectively, the old reading strategies have become habits. All habits receive dopamine reinforcement in the **nucleus accumbens** (reward pathway) whenever they are completed. When dopamine is secreted in the reward pathway, you subconsciously feel better, improving your homeostasis. The absence of dopamine at expected times will produce subconscious dissatisfaction and lower emotional balance.

Applying the new strategies will utilize high brain energy. Because the brain cannot engage in actions requiring high energy for an extended period, it will require periods of respite when engaging in the new action to regain energy. The result is that engaging in new tasks, even if they are easy, produces a higher level of fatigue. Implementing the new strategies will seem exhausting when you are stressed or tired. You will subconsciously be less satisfied with the new strategies because you are doing something other than the old action that provided a dopamine boost. As the pace of the school year begins to increase, making the workday more demanding, the brain will seek the ease of old habits and desire to reclaim the lost dopamine. You will soon become discontented with the new strategies and are likely to regress to old habits. A negative view toward the new strategies will increase, and the rational brain will identify a list of reasons why the new strategies are inefficient and ineffective. If individuals knew that consistent practice of any new behavior would eventually get easier and receive dopamine, more people would show greater fortitude.

> *Engaging in new tasks, even if they are easy, produces a higher level of fatigue.*

Think of life as a software update. Most of us dislike updates because we have become versed in operating the old software system. However, we must continue using the updates, and over a short period of time, we grow accustomed to the changes, and all is forgotten until the next update. The unfortunate fact is that most changes do not require consistent practice, and we are able to retreat. Imagine if software updates offered people the ability to choose whether to update or keep the old operating system; how many people would still be using MS-DOS, Microsoft's first operating system?

Let's revisit the new reading program. Supervisors assessing the implementation of the new strategies will notice that more and more staff are not carrying out the new interventions. They will likely interpret this behavior as staff being resistant to change. Suppose the school has experienced a pattern of failed initiatives. In that case, staff failing to maintain the new practice is anticipated, and the new reading program will soon be unceremoniously buried in the expansive graveyard of past failed programs. Understanding why most new programs fail has given rise to implementation science. **Implementation science** is a field that attempts to gain a better understanding of how the brain can achieve long-term change.

Give in to Hyperbole

Negativity bias lends itself to more elaborate retelling than positive events. The phenomenon is due to the brain giving greater emphasis to the negative and the level of emotion that is triggered. Many people perceive emotional memory is as consistent as recalling learned facts: 1 + 1 = 2. However, emotional memories are re-created every time we remember them and migrate toward emotions held. As a result, each retelling of a negative experience can change without our knowledge because we cannot compare it to earlier recounting. One study found that a negativity bias principle is that when we recall negative experiences, our vocabulary tends to become richer and more varied than what was depicted earlier (Peeters, 1971).

> *Emotional memories are re-created every time we remember them and migrate toward emotions held.*

The principle that negative memories tend to become worse over time has far-reaching implications. One obvious outcome is that our response to a negative event will become justified. For example, if we respond inappropriately to something or someone, recalling the event will become more egregious and better support our poor behavior. Another implication is that negative events often produce ripples. Because negative events are so weighted in the brain, the retelling of negative information is more likely to be retold by those hearing it and becomes worse as the story spreads. Negative bias reduces the ability to implement change because one negative outcome related to the change usually spreads, reducing the probability of success. Although research found that the memory of adverse events intensifies over time, the same study found that positive events do not morph in a similar manner (McGaugh, 2000). The result is that good outcomes related to a new initiative do not spread like negative outcomes, which means that a positive ripple is unlikely.

> *Negative bias reduces the ability to implement change because one negative outcome related to the change usually spreads, reducing the probability of success.*

Be on the Lookout

Negative stimuli carry greater informational value than positive stimuli. Thus, positive information requires greater attention and cognitive processing (Peeters & Czapinski, 1990). We spend more time looking at negative than positive stimuli (Ducette & Soucar, 1974; Fiske, 1980). Anyone who has made a presentation and reviewed the participant evaluations knows firsthand how we weigh negative input. You had 45 participants: Most rated the session as good to excellent; however, one individual thought it was poor and made some negative comments. The rest of the day, those negative comments intruded into your thoughts, yet you did not revisit any of the positive comments made by the other participants. Negative bias plays a more significant role in judgment and decision-making. Whenever one is making determinations, negative aspects are weighted more heavily than positive aspects (Kahneman & Tversky, 1984; Peeters & Czapinski, 1990). Therefore, a conscious decision to look for the positive is required by a good decision-maker. Imagine always making critical decisions with biased information. No rational person would say that only looking at partial information is the best way to make sound decisions. However, we do precisely that every day. Whenever we fail to see the positive that exists and only focus on the negative, we bias our thought processes. Negative stimuli already receive such a significantly higher level of attention, activation, and emotional response by the human brain that noticing the positive aspects of any situation is not enough. We must be aware of our brain's tendency to skew us toward the negative, and we need to balance that fact when reaching crucial decisions.

RECOMMENDATIONS FOR EDUCATORS

1. Practice the Mindfulness Condition

What it is: The **mindfulness condition** refers to the ability to maintain a moment-by-moment awareness of your thoughts, feelings, bodily sensations, and surrounding environment through a more positive lens. Participants in the mindfulness condition demonstrated less negativity bias in attitude formation (Kiken & Shook, 2011). That is, they correctly classified positive and negative stimuli more equally than those in the control condition. Interestingly, the difference in negativity bias stemmed from better categorization of positives. Furthermore, those who can maintain a mindfulness condition reported higher levels of optimism compared to the control condition. Together, these results suggest that mindfulness increases positive judgments and reduces negativity bias.

What it looks like in practice:

- A simple exercise that can help students develop a mindfulness condition is having them take notice of their environment and attempt to view it from a positive perspective. For example, your plane is delayed, and your plans to visit your family are dramatically altered. You can view your plans as irrevocably ruined and your vacation a disaster, or you can tell yourself that nobody can control the weather and you will make the best of the situation when you arrive at your destination.

- Another mindfulness technique is to have students be present in the moment—mental grounding. Have students focus on a few things in the immediate environment and attempt to note every detail they see. This simple action shifts the mind from other distractions, and when completed, the students are better able to focus on what will come next.

Why it works: One of the most valuable lessons we can teach students is that they can overcome harmful life circumstances by learning to view them from a better perspective. Perspective determines how the brain views the world and dictates how you respond to events. This is not teaching students to be unrealistic; it is helping them to learn that your perspective alters your brain and body chemistry. A positive perspective improves homeostasis and helps students learn to control their emotions better. Emotional control can be increased dramatically if a student can learn to view life events from a better perspective consistently.

2. **Model Supportive Relationships**

What it is: Teachers should be aware of the effects of negative bias on student–teacher and student–student relationships. It is important for teachers to remember the importance of affect on the brain. We are programmed to notice nonverbal emotional expressions and overemphasize negative expressions.

What it looks like in practice:

- Create a positive classroom climate in which teachers and students are supportive of one another by consistently projecting a positive attitude. Teachers can help students develop supportive habits. For example, whenever a student gets an answer correct, the class responds with three claps. Students are encouraged by their peers and are motivated to answer correctly.

- Don't let one negative event influence your long-term opinion of a student. Teachers should admit that a pronounced negative incident with a student is likely to impact the ability to cultivate or maintain a relationship with said student. The teacher first needs to acknowledge what she is feeling concerning the student; awareness helps us address emotions more calmly. Then the teacher should attempt to identify the positive qualities the student possesses. This step forces the brain not to only focus on the negative. One of the best strategies is for the teacher to ask and then imagine the best positive outcome for this student in her class this year. This strategy allows the teacher's brain to shift focus from what can go wrong to what could go well.

- Instruction and grading should reflect encouragement. Encouragement does not mean false praise; rather, it means looking for something the student did well or showing potential even when not meeting academic or behavioral standards. Most of us dread seeing the color red when getting a test back. Red highlighted our mistakes. However, a teacher can select another color that highlights things the student did well. Imagine getting an essay back with the red correction and green notations highlighting the essay's strengths.

Why it works: Knowing negative bias's impact on relationships can help teachers take a more contemplative rather than emotional view of incidents that can hinder student–teacher relationships. Success is naturally motivating to the human brain. Criticism hampers motivation. Instruction should walk the fine line of correcting in a non-negative manner. For example, once a student demonstrates repeated negative behaviors, the subconscious movements of our eyes will monitor that student more closely, thus increasing the likelihood that more negative behaviors are seen and addressed than with other students in the class. Teachers who understand the impact negative bias has on student monitoring can intentionally attempt to positively reinforce students' behavior when they are on task. The need to be positive is especially true for students who have experienced repeated academic and behavioral failure.

3. Positive Training

What it is: We are so disposed toward the negative that many of us need to train our brains to be more positive and find the balance we need to live healthy and productive lives. Many strategies for producing a more positive brain have been researched and validated. Dr. Richard Davidson, the co-author of *The Emotional Life of Your Brain*, conducted fascinating experiments on treating depression by better understanding how to engage in behaviors that positively stimulate the brain. Davidson found that by learning what stimulates the left prefrontal cortex, we can train people to be happier, and by learning what calms the right prefrontal cortex, we can reduce sadness and negativity (Davidson & Begley, 2012). He found that people can train contentment by improving their *awareness*, *connection*, *insight*, and *purpose*.

What it looks like in practice:

- Davidson defines **awareness** as the ability to remain in the present by paying attention to your surroundings, being self-aware, and being focused. Many people would recognize this as a mindfulness technique.

- **Connection** in this context refers to emotions that underpin successful relationships with others. The emphasis here is on acts of kindness, empathy, and maintaining a positive outlook.

- **Insight** refers to having a healthy sense of self and the ability to both reframe self-defeating narratives and bounce back quickly from adverse events. There are data that demonstrate people who have practiced meditation for many years essentially rewire their brain's ability to engage in emotional regulation (Lutz et al., 2004). This can also be called **resiliency**. Davidson's research supports the findings that resilient people demonstrate a high level of self-regulation. Also, improvements in resiliency correlated to improved brain function. For example, resiliency studies found that one critical protective factor in becoming more resilient is having a long-term positive relationship—which directly increases oxytocin levels in the brain (Schneiderman et al., 2012). Oxytocin lowers stress and helps the prefrontal cortex better control emotions.

- **Purpose** in life is having a belief that life has meaning; people who believe that their life has purpose recover from negative events and even live longer. Davidson cited a study of people in their 70s and 80s, finding that those with less sense of purpose in life died earlier (Davidson & Lutz, 2008).

Why it works: It is more critical today than ever to be mindful because so many people are constantly distracted from the present by their cell phones. A study from 2012 found that 47% of American adults do not pay attention to what they are doing at any given moment. The study concluded that people report being less happy when not paying attention (Davidson & Begley, 2012). Another way of looking at being aware is that it is a proven strategy for increasing focus and strengthening the prefrontal cortex. Davidson found that meditation that focused on compassion increased warm-heartedness and altruism, which he related to changes in brain function. The association of meditation with improved brain function is not a leap because many studies have documented improvements in body and brain functions in monks who consistently engaged in meditation (Davidson & Lutz, 2008; Lutz et al., 2006).

What it looks like in practice: Another school of thought comes from Shawn Achor, the author of *The Happiness Advantage*. He found that your success rate will increase if you can find ways to become more positive. According to Achor, 90% of your happiness is based not on your external world but on your internal world. In terms of success, 75% is based on your optimism and your social support, and becoming more positive doesn't have to take a lot of time. Anchor posits that people may be able to retrain their brain by doing as little as 2 minutes of activities consistently for only 21 days in a row. I caution people not to take exact amounts of time to rewire the brain literally but rather to take them as an estimate based on a sample of individuals.

Achor cites the following retraining activities (Achor, 2010).

- Gratitude Exercises. Write down three things you are grateful for over the last 24 hours. They can be very simple things that matter to you. For example, I was up at dawn today and saw the sunrise, which always makes me smile.

- The Doubler. Take one positive experience from the past 24 hours and spend 2 minutes writing down every detail about that experience. When you make this practice a habit, your brain begins to identify these events as valuable, and you will notice other similar events.

- The Fun Fifteen. Do 15 minutes of fun cardio activity, like gardening or walking the dog, every day. The effects of daily cardio can be as effective as taking an antidepressant.

- Meditation. Every day take 2 minutes to stop whatever you are doing and concentrate on breathing.

- Conscious act of kindness. At the start of every day, send a short email or text praising someone you know.

- Deepen Social Connections. Spend time with family and friends.

Why it works: Social connections are one of the best predictors of success, health, and even life expectancy. They promote oxytocin, which helps us regulate stress. Our brains become addicted to feeling good by making others feel good. Even a short mindful break can result in a calmer, happier you. Many people find it challenging to become more positive. However, consistent behaviors rewire the brain. Engaging in any of these positive actions will help your brain better balance the positive with the negative. The practice of being more positive will improve cognitive and physical functions and quality of life as well.

CONCLUSION

Change is often difficult due to new behaviors consuming higher brain energy and the loss of dopamine from the loss of established habits. Educators should accept that how we usually react to change is emotional. The emotional process of the brain precedes the logical process. As a result, we need to identify that the initial reaction to change is likely to be negative and emotional. In addition, we should try to look at positive outcomes and evaluate them fairly. The process that should be adapted is to engage in the new action until we get used to it. Once we do this, less energy will be required, and dopamine will reinforce the practice. Additionally, educators should be aware that students are also experiencing and struggling with change.

CHAPTER 3

··

BELIEVE IT OR NOT
Confirmation Bias

CHAPTER OVERVIEW

▶ The brain is programmed to see things in the environment that support existing beliefs. The implication is that what we believe concerning student behavior and performance will likely be confirmed. Research shows that teachers' beliefs about students might be the strongest predictor of outcomes. The sad truth is that confirmation bias not only confirms what we believe but tends to impose that belief on students. However, knowing how confirmation bias is produced allows teachers to mitigate the negative outcomes the bias can produce.

BIAS AND OUR BELIEF SYSTEM

Confirmation bias refers to the brain's tendency to notice things in our environment that support our beliefs and values, while missing contradictions in front of us. The missing of contradictions is not intentional. Confirmation bias works in conjunction with our microsaccades. **Microsaccades** are constant scanning motions of the eyes (Xue et al., 2020), and they serve many functions: They are constantly scanning to divert our attention toward threats and desires within our field of vision (Martinez-Conde & Macknik, 2007). Our ability to fix our attention at one point makes us vulnerable to things happening on our peripherals. The ability to hold attention and scan our environment simultaneously keeps us safe. Microsaccades scan for things we desire in our environment, which is also related to survival. The ability to notice someone we are attracted to and desire to mate with perpetuates humanity. It is thought that microsaccades have evolved to include a range of personal desires. Therefore, if you have a powerful weakness for chocolate cake and enter a room where a decadent chocolate fudge cake is in a discrete corner, odds are you will not miss it.

Microsaccades also work in conjunction with our implicit biases. This is why we are prone to noticing negative things in our environment. A clear example of how microsaccades function in relation to bias happens when we read. Our eyes notice negative words faster and linger on them milliseconds longer than when coming across positive words. Microsaccades work similarly when we encounter things that can confirm our beliefs and values. Because we are wired to notice certain things, other items often go unobserved. As a result, confirmation bias can appear intentional to the casual observer. A person with a strong bias might miss a contradiction apparent to most of the others in the room. The natural conclusion is that the person is so biased that they willfully ignore alternative data. What makes confirmation bias perplexing is that two individuals with strong opposing viewpoints notice all the evidence the other is missing, further escalating emotions and entrenching positions. No wonder researchers have concluded that confirmation bias is one of the leading causes of polarization between groups of differing beliefs (Myers,

1982; Sunstein, 2002). Consider some of the major issues that polarize America. Both sides of global warming and the environment, education, abortion, foreign trade, immigration, gun laws, the government's role in providing health care, and income tax fairness point to examples that can be seen to support their position. Each side is equally enraged at their opponent's unwillingness to notice the daily examples that justify their positions. Not surprisingly, confirmation bias is seen as the leading cause of a significant portion of disputes, altercations, and misunderstandings among individuals, groups, and nations (Koriat et al., 1980).

> *Confirmation bias is one of the leading causes of polarization between groups of differing beliefs (Myers, 1982; Sunstein, 2002).*

> *Confirmation bias is seen as the leading cause of a significant portion of disputes, altercations, and misunderstandings among individuals, groups, and nations (Koriat et al., 1980).*

Expert vs. Novice

An indicator of an individual's level of confirmation bias is their confidence in their positions. Research has found that a high level of confidence increases an individual's tendency to reason away or reject alternative points of view (Mercier, 2016). There is a difference between an expert and a novice. It is far more rational for someone who is accomplished in math and has achieved notoriety in their chosen field to have a high degree of confidence in their opinions on math. However, if that individual has a similar level of confidence in a wide range of other subjects, it indicates confirmation bias on a wide range of topics. Confidence is not consistently correlated with knowledge or intelligence. We have all met individuals who are experts in everything, hold extreme opinions, and will argue and dismiss people who are experts on a topic.

It is important to note that being an expert does not prevent confirmation bias in a person's chosen field. Studies show that confirmation bias is widespread among professionals who are supposed to be searching for objective truths, such as judges, scientists, and physicians (Nickerson, 1998). The issue is that our beliefs become an early filter for all incoming information. Confirmation bias occurs within 200 milliseconds before contradictory information reaches our prefrontal cortex. Therefore, we are influenced before information is considered. Emotional experiences reduce prefrontal cortex activation, which explains why beliefs that we are emotional about are seldom rationally reconsidered. The result is that intelligent, fair-minded individuals can be oblivious to their biases. We are all motivated to make rational arguments for whatever we believe, unaware that we are prone not to consider existing or new vital information.

Update Pending . . .

Most people are unaware that we are internally motivated not to modify our beliefs.

Researchers observed that the **posterior cingulate cortex** is activated when we face new information that challenges existing beliefs. The amazing finding was that once we maintain our belief, dopamine activates, rewarding the act of holding our existing position (Westen et al., 2006). When dopamine is released in the reward pathway, it makes us subconsciously feel better. Over time, we develop a habitual pattern of not amending beliefs, values, or positions because holding on to them makes us feel good. Most of us are unaware that holding on to existing beliefs is chemically reinforced. The dilemma is that making good decisions requires updating beliefs according to new evidence. Confirmation bias reduces our ability to update our beliefs. Even more problematic is that, when beliefs become entrenched, they become resistant to new evidence. In more extreme cases, we become enraged by new evidence. The two most common results are attacking the people who hold opposing viewpoints and seeking out those who validate our beliefs. Social media may have created confirmation bias on steroids. For the first time in history, we can find infinite voices that support even the most outlandish theories. In a matter of minutes, we can identify hundreds of sites that support our beliefs, strengthening our biases and providing a false sense of mainstream support.

> *Confirmation bias reduces our ability to update our beliefs.*

There are both healthy and unhealthy levels of belief. Individuals prone to conspiracy theories, myths, and the paranormal demonstrate genetic differences in dopamine neurotransmission associated with their perceptions and belief maintenance (Schmack et al., 2015). In these cases, maintaining and voicing their beliefs can become a form of self-medication. For example, many emotional disorders share a similar feature: dopamine deficit. It is often referred to as reward deficit syndrome. **Reward deficit syndrome** is a lower secretion of dopamine in the nucleus accumbens. The triggering of dopamine in the nucleus accumbens enables us to develop healthy habits. Once we engage in a behavior for a short period of time, dopamine secretes, motivating us to maintain the behavior. For example, many adults make their beds in the morning. This behavior likely began in childhood because we were told to do it by our parents. Once the behavior was done consistently for a short time, dopamine began to secrete whenever the practice was completed. The dopamine subconsciously rewards the behavior and improves the brain's chemical disposition. Without this reinforcement, we could not fall into healthy patterns such as a morning routine and going to work.

People with reward deficit syndrome tend not to get dopamine when engaging in behaviors that should become habits. It is the secretion of dopamine that helps us to become disciplined and consistent in our daily routines. Those who do not secrete dopamine when engaging in daily practices struggle to develop healthy habits and must resort to more extreme behaviors to trigger the dopamine response. The same thing holds for individuals who maintain extreme beliefs. They seem to have progressed to more extreme positions because every time they voice their belief, they receive dopamine reinforcement. Eventually, dopamine lowers, forcing them to adopt an even more extreme position or voice their beliefs more frequently. We have all met individuals who will share their extreme beliefs with anyone. Most individuals can read a person's level of interest in what another person is sharing, but those suffering from reward deficit syndrome can get to the point that they share their beliefs no longer for others to consider but rather to get their dopamine needs met. This explains the person who does not care that the majority rejects their beliefs; they are, in a way, self-medicating.

Confirmation bias is evident not only when protecting strong beliefs but also when we reach even insignificant conclusions. As a result, we tend to interpret new information in a way that supports any past conclusion. A study asked participants if the dots on a screen moved clockwise or counterclockwise on two occasions. After making their initial decision about the direction the dots were moving in the first experiment, the participants were more likely to see them moving in the same direction in the subsequent experiment, even if they were not moving (Talluri et al., 2018). The researchers concluded that confirmation bias is evident in inconsequential decisions. The reality is that our days are full of confirming things we believe that are not true.

Foundational Studies

Perhaps no better example of how confirmation bias influences education is provided by Rosenthal and Jacobson. In 1966, students across the country were given IQ tests at the beginning of the first grade, and the scores were provided to their teachers. Rosenthal and Jacobson told teachers at an elementary school that their students had taken a new test called the Harvard Test of Inflected Acquisition, which predicted which students would improve the most academically in the coming year. However, no such test existed. In 18 classes from Grades 1 through 6, teachers were given lists of the students who had scored in the top 20% on the Harvard Test. These students were identified as "intellectual bloomers" with the highest expectations of academic growth. The truth was that the students identified as intellectually superior were randomly selected. Eight months later, all students were given a second IQ test in addition to the one they had taken before the beginning of the school year.

Generally, all students designated as potential bloomers had significantly greater gains in IQ scores than those not identified as bloomers (Rosenthal & Jacobson, 1992). This experiment illustrates that IQ is not set, and changes correlate to academic progress. In addition, the students identified as "intellectual bloomers" also demonstrated the most academic growth compared with students not identified as intellectually superior.

Two years later, Schrank conducted a similar experiment, which showed that teacher beliefs are consistently confirmed. Schrank told teachers their classes grouped students with particularly high or low learning potential. High-potential grouped students consistently outperformed the low-potential grouped students (Schrank, 1968). However, as in the Rosenthal and Jacobson experiment, the groupings were random. The adverse effects of confirmation bias are often overlooked in these experiments. In both experiments, very gifted students were arbitrarily identified as low performers and consistently performed below their capacity based on being identified as performing poorly on intelligence tests. In 1985, Brophy confirmed the power of negative expectations on student performance. He showed that false evaluation of student capacity lowered student performance and, more importantly, harmed student motivation (Brophy, 1985). Brophy found eight teacher behaviors produced by low expectations: giving up easily on low-expectation students; criticizing them more often for failure; praising them less often following success; praising inappropriately; neglecting to give them any feedback following their responses; seating them in the back of the room; generally paying less attention to them or interacting with them less frequently; and expressing less warmth toward them or less interest in them as individuals.

All these studies illustrate how teacher beliefs impact student performance. When teachers can maintain positive expectations concerning students, expectations are often met. Teachers should condition themselves to be on the lookout for evidence of positive student potential and achievement. Confirming positive examples and conditioning the brain to see the potential in each student will maximize opportunities for success.

Emotional Memories

Emotional memories are re-created and move in the direction of our beliefs.

How we emotionally react to a specific event or situation the first time can affect how memories change when we recall them later (Kensinger & Schacter, 2008). The moment we experience a belief concerning an event ensures that the memories of the event will continually morph to emphasize the belief more. Emotional memories fall prey to accuracy-confidence and are more likely to change over time (Dougal & Rotello, 2007; Jonsson et al., 2005; Schmolck et al., 2000). We are unaware that our memories are changing because we cannot compare a past memory to a present one. Each time we re-create an emotional memory, it is the only version we are cognizant of.

How we emotionally react to a specific event or situation the first time can affect how memories change when we recall them later (Kensinger & Schacter, 2008).

For example, you and your younger sister are going away for a girls' weekend. No kids and no husbands, hooray! After unpacking, you settle on the deck to enjoy a bottle of wine and exchange childhood stories. Suddenly, your sister's countenance changes, and with tears in her eyes, she confesses that she has been bothered by an event that transpired when you were children. Concerned, you inquire what it is. She proceeds to tell you about an incident that happened when you were 13 and she was 10. You put her down in front of all your friends at a party, proclaiming loudly that all her ideas were stupid. She ran out of the party crying and devastated. You quickly apologize and bring to her attention that you were 13. Your sister says you have always put down her ideas since that day. She proceeds to give you a list of examples: Some you remember, some you remember differently, and others you are convinced never happened. The issue is that your sister's initial memory has changed to support her belief better. That belief becomes a filter of all future events. Any time your behavior can be interpreted to support that belief, the position is confirmed and strengthened. All those memories are likely also to change, making her initial assertion irrefutable in her eyes.

From irrelevant beliefs to significant ones, confirmation bias determines what we see and strengthens our existing positions. Most of us go through life blissfully unaware of how wrong many of our assertions are. Therefore, we seldom reevaluate our beliefs and are amazed when people believe differently. It is easy to understand that from the certainty produced by confirmation bias, brothers argue with brothers, groups are opposed to other groups, and nations are rooted in conflict with other nations. However, those who know how confirmation bias works are comfortable that we can be right yet wrong.

> *Confirmation bias determines what we see and strengthens our existing positions.*

RECOMMENDATIONS FOR EDUCATORS

1. Establish and Maintain High Student Expectations

What it is: We need to accept that we do not challenge our beliefs; we need to look for contradictory evidence. Negative bias and confirmation bias are powerful allies. When our beliefs are negative, they intensify quickly under mounting evidence we are adept at uncovering. When teachers believe negative things about students, it is improbable that the students can overcome the assertion.

What it looks like in practice:

- Once a student is identified as a low academic performer or having a behavior problem, microsaccades will monitor those students more closely for any demonstration of the presenting problem. The higher level of monitoring will result in increased negative feedback. The teacher should be intentional in checking in on those students.

- And, if the students are on task during scheduled check-ins, the teacher should reinforce the behavior.

Why it works: Two of the most significant predictors of student success are high expectations and a positive relationship with the student. Knowing how confirmation bias works helps teachers put into practice strategies that can minimize the adverse outcomes of confirmation bias. It is important to remember that confirmation bias occurs at a subconscious level prior to awareness. The issue is not intention but awareness.

2. **Be Cognizant of How Confirmation Bias Influences Teacher–Student Relationships**

What it is: There is an element of confirmation bias that promotes a self-fulfilling prophecy. Positive student perceptions increase good outcomes, and negative views concerning students lead to poor outcomes. Therefore, negative options concerning a student have a range of ramifications. It will alter what the teacher will notice, further solidifying existing options. Confirmation bias also alters our attitudes toward the student, increasing the probability that they will behave as expected.

What it looks like in practice:

- Be intentional about identifying contradictory evidence that can balance negative beliefs about a student. In addition to being on the lookout for positive behavior, teachers can seek out the opinions of other adults who have a better relationship with the student. Hearing alternative perspectives concerning a student enables the mind to spot what others say about a student.

- Override the impact by recalling something positive you have learned about the student whenever the bad thought occurs (Grella et al., 2022).

- Create opportunities for the student to put their best foot forward in order to change the perspective of both teacher and student. Studies have found that taking on a cooperative mindset is a proven strategy for reducing confirmation bias (Schwind & Buder, 2012). Merely taking on the mindset of "How can I overcome this opinion of the student in order that they can be more successful?" has been shown to reduce the impact of confirmation bias.

- Be aware that emotional memories are constantly shifting. People unwittingly add false details to their memories that further support what they believe to be true. The fact that memories shift over time is so established that it has been verified in hundreds of studies (Loftus, 2005). Educators need to be aware that false enhancements of an event occur more often for negative experiences than positive ones (Kensinger, 2009).

- Write down the facts of an emotional incident without too much commentary and then review the notes when recalling the incident. This simple exercise seems to temper the movement of memories from becoming an emotionally driven story to reviewing the facts. There is even evidence that the act of writing down the emotions felt during an incident can be therapeutic and reduce the related stress and trauma (Pennebaker, 2017).

Why it works: The most intense confirmation biases are usually born of negative emotional experiences. Due to confirmation bias, adverse incidents that trigger emotions are usually rapport killers between teacher and student. The most sinister outcome of a confirmation bias is that it prevents students from improving. The first rule of psychology is that you get more of what you reinforce. Teachers motivated to see students improve would be devastated to know that they are complicit in one student's failure.

CONCLUSION

The powerful lesson that confirmation bias teaches us is that teacher expectations are usually fulfilled. This can be an encouraging lesson because high expectations consistently yield improved performance. The critical element is belief. When teachers believe that all students can excel, it influences what their eyes focus on and alters behaviors. Teachers who believe in their students produce students who believe in themselves.

CHAPTER 4

....

MAXIMUM IMPACT

Impact Bias

CHAPTER OVERVIEW

► Impact bias refers to our tendency to predict the outcomes of possible future events and magnify how an incident will make us feel. Since impact bias is intricately linked to emotions, our predictions are usually overblown. The stronger the expected emotions, the more they will influence our behavior. Impact bias plays a significant role in schools' inability to implement and sustain change. Any staff member who feels negatively toward the change will predict the worst and subconsciously participate in helping validate their predictions.

IMPACT BIAS

Impact bias is our tendency to overestimate the emotional impact of future events. The result is that good events are imagined to be epic, and bad events are expected to be traumatic; thus, we miscalculate both the intensity and the duration of future events. Most of us began to experience the tendency to overestimate the emotional impact of future events as children. Remember that Christmas gift that was supposed to change your life? Christmas Day finally arrived, and you woke your parents at the crack of dawn. You tore open the gift and screamed in excitement—you got it! But by noon, you were bored because it was not endless fun like they promised in the commercials. Perhaps the most salient point is that this experience and others like it did not deter you from inflating the value of other future events. An aspect of impact bias seems to blind us to the fact that we repeatedly engage in the practice.

> *Impact bias seems to blind us to the fact that we repeatedly engage in the practice.*

Humans are the only creatures on the earth who can predict what will happen well into the future. Because we can make predictions, we tend to create scenarios: If this happens, then that will happen. Sometimes, we make complex scenarios, with each future event becoming more catastrophic. Before we know it, we have become stressed and anxious concerning events that are not likely to happen.

MOTIVATION

All automated functions are rooted in survival. For example, we pay little attention to our heart rate and breathing because the brain has become so efficient with those functions. Since impact bias is a survival function, we don't notice our tendency to overestimate the impact of change in our lives. Many researchers fail to see the value of impact bias because it heightens emotions and leads to bad decision-making. When we make future decisions based on temporary feelings, we magnify the importance of insignificant factors and are, therefore, more likely to make ineffective choices. However, Morewedge's research found that the primary purpose of impact bias is motivation. In a series of experiments, he found that once we forecast the future, we are committed to producing it (Morewedge & Buechel, 2013). Forecasters were even more likely to exhibit impact bias when they believed they could influence future outcomes. For example, athletes who predicted a high emotional toll if they lost a race consistently worked harder to avoid defeats (Van Dijk, 2009). However, individuals who utilize pessimistic predictions as a primary source of motivation can find themselves exaggerating the adverse outcomes and experiencing not motivation, but instead paralysis. Their predictions become so dire that they cannot think or act because they are overcome with panic or fear of failure. More and more students who perceive themselves as being under pressure to achieve academically begin to make poor decisions such as cheating or taking performance-enhancing drugs. Others may succumb to the pressure and experience emotional complications such as panic attacks and mood disorders.

> *The primary purpose of impact bias is motivation.*

Impact bias is meant to give individuals a greater sense of control over the future. Researchers found that impact bias is more pronounced in people who have made a prediction than in individuals who have made no forecast (Morewedge & Buechel, 2013). The researchers found that the effort to engage in behaviors that will make a prediction become a reality is directly proportional to the level of belief that it will come true. Humans need to feel a sense of control over events that feel uncontrollable. This ability might play a role in maintaining **homeostasis**, or maintaining equilibrium. Humans are motivated to avoid events that can cause them emotional discomfort.

THE STRUGGLES OF COMPLEXITY

Based on our experiences, we can accurately predict the emotions we will experience in some specific circumstances. For example, we know that comedy is more likely to produce laughter than sadness, or watching our team win a championship will result in joy rather than disappointment (Robinson & Clore, 2001). The ability to accurately predict emotions in many circumstances has resulted in a false sense of certainty in more complex situations. Most of life is not lived on a one-dimensional playing field. Emotions can occur in complex blends, and people often fail to anticipate the precise mixture of feelings they will experience. Research has shown that more complicated events can produce a combination of positive and negative emotions (Robinson & Clore, 2001). When people predict a complex future, they tend to predict their emotions simplistically. This is especially true for events with a wide range of variables and outcomes. Research on impact bias found that the more distant a prediction is in the future, the more overly simplistic the emotional schema (Larsen et al., 2001). Further complicating matters, people often misconstrue complex social situations when imagining them in advance, making the predictions of future emotions less reliable (Woodzicka & LaFrance, 2001). When predicting how a future event will make us feel, we tend to overestimate how quickly the emotion will be felt, how intense the emotion will be, and how long the emotion will last.

> *More complicated events can produce a combination of positive and negative emotions (Robinson & Clore, 2001).*

Wilson and Gilbert identified two human tendencies that contribute to the inaccuracy of predicting the impact of future events:

1. When we predict that a future event will significantly alter our emotional stability, we tend to exhibit tunnel vision (T. Wilson & Gilbert, 2005).

2. We have a tendency to rationalize life events (T. Wilson & Gilbert, 2005).

When people think about the impact of future events, they tend to forget about what else is going on in their lives that might be influencing their emotional state at that moment. For example, people experiencing stress tend to anticipate a more stressful future. The reality is that human emotions are not compartmentalized, and future events are influenced by present events. We conveniently forget that the future is uncertain, and what we feel today may not be our future emotional condition.

> *People experiencing stress tend to anticipate a more stressful future.*

When something bad happens, we immediately search for the underlying reasons. Once we identify the underlying reasons, we start to feel better. Humans struggle with uncertainty, and even when something terrible happens, a rational explanation reduces the feelings of fear and the random nature of unexplained adverse events. It is unfortunate that we do the same thing with unexpected positive events—we rationalize them, which reduces the positive impact on the brain. The reason is that when we experience positive feelings, wonderful chemicals flood the brain. The moment we rationalize an event, we activate the prefrontal cortex, reducing activity in the brain's limbic region. It is within the limbic region that the amygdala configures emotional chemical responses.

WHY CHANGE IS HARD

Change is hard because it challenges our homeostasis, the body's ability to maintain a state of equilibrium within the external environment. Our minds and bodies adapt over time to the organizational structure we are consistently exposed to. Research shows that organizational consistency plays a crucial role in maintaining homeostasis, and as a result, we desire to maintain these patterns and resist change (Regev et al., 2013). Since change negatively impacts our equilibrium at a biological level, most change triggers negative emotions in most staff. As a result, school administrators should be aware that implementing change is difficult because it causes chemical upheaval in the mind and body, triggering emotions.

The moment negative emotions are triggered related to change, impact bias will occur. The greater the level of emotional disturbance, the more extreme the anticipated impact. The predicted negative outcome produces stress and anxiety concerning events that may not happen. The idea that organizational change increases stress and anxiety has been proven (Wisse & Sleebos, 2016). The low success rate of organizational change has been directly linked to the emotional toll staff perceive during change initiatives (Fugate et al., 2012). This means that before most change is allowed to succeed, most staff subconsciously seek to restore organizational structures to the patterns to which their minds and bodies have grown accustomed. Then, without conscious effort or malicious intent, they will subconsciously engage in behaviors that will make their predictions come true. The staff response will look like resistance to change to the school administrator. However, school administrators and educators who know how the brain tends to respond can proactively plan to implement change more successfully.

Educators should know that the mind and body maintain homeostasis best in predictable and supportive environments (Leong, 2024). This means that one of the best indicators of the ability to support change is if you have established a predictable environment. Although change will still cause some disruption to homeostasis, a school environment that maintains enough routines and rituals will restore balance quickly. Also, stress is a natural disruptor of homeostasis. Therefore, implementing change through a supportive and gradual approach promotes homeostasis.

When implementing change, the school administrator should anticipate impact bias and proactively address the most common issues. There are two critical steps to combating impact bias. One is getting staff to understand that although we can predict what will happen in the future, most predictions are unreliable. If we could accurately predict the future, our lives would be dramatically different. The second step is getting staff to understand that there are many valid ways to achieve a goal. Therefore, most change initiatives select one of many valid methods. If staff can accept that there are many ways to achieve a goal, they can suspend the belief that an alternative approach is better. This can be achieved by simply having staff brainstorm all the valid approaches to achieve the desired change. When staff can suspend their beliefs and accept that the proposed change is a valid approach to achieving the desired change, they can get behind it. Educators should be aware that studies on implementing school change have shown that the greatest predictor of successfully implementing any new initiative is when most staff members can get behind the change and believe it will work (Meyer et al., 2023).

RECOMMENDATIONS FOR EDUCATORS

1. Realize That We Cannot Predict the Future

What it means: When does confirmation bias impact education the most? Whenever education attempts to make a change. Change is hard for the human brain and can often trigger strong emotions, causing impact bias to predict severe outcomes. As a result, many people predict an unfavorable outcome because of the change. Once a negative prediction has occurred, we subconsciously work to make our predictions come true.

What it looks like in practice: When schools attempt to implement change, they should consider doing two activities with staff.

- Have each person write down what they predict will occur because of the change. Have them put the prediction into an envelope, seal it, and put their name on it. After everyone has completed that exercise, brainstorm with staff all of the valid scenarios that could occur if the change is implemented.

- Three months into the change, reconvene the staff, return their sealed envelopes, and have them read their predictions. Then, once again, have staff brainstorm all the possible scenarios that could now happen related to the change being implemented.

Why it works: The exercise reinforces that our predictions are not infallible and can be very wrong. Also, many scenarios can happen, and the behavior of humans influences the direction. When this exercise is repeated whenever a change is attempted, educators will begin to reflect that their predictions can be wrong. In addition, they will begin to be open to the fact that there are many possible future scenarios. This awareness is essential because once the brain is married to one scenario, it often fails to consider other alternatives.

2. Reflect on the Past

What it means: When individuals focus solely on future events that produce some emotional anticipation, impact bias will take hold.

What it looks like in practice:

- When we focus on relevant past experiences related to change, the brain can be realistic and mute outlandish emotional predictions (Buehler & McFarland, 2001).

1. Think of similar past experiences that had positive outcomes. For example, the school is implementing a new curriculum. Five years ago, you had to learn a new curriculum, and at first, it was hard, but it improved student outcomes.

2. Remember crisis experiences that ended up being a blessing in disguise. For example, you lost your job and were forced into a new career path that you are now passionate about.

3. Recall changes that increased your resiliency or competencies. For example, you were diagnosed with a medical issue, and as a result, you transformed your eating and exercise habits and are healthier than you have ever been.

4. Reflect on similar past events before predicting the future. For example, your school is adopting a peer collaboration model for lesson planning, and you recall a similar grade-level team approach for creating lessons at the first school you worked at that was successful.

Why it works: Researchers found that having participants focus on future events they thought would produce strong emotions like happiness or fear increased impact bias. As their predictions of future scenarios became more outlandish, the anticipated emotion became more intense. However, when they got participants to focus on relevant past experiences, future scenarios became more realistic, and emotional anticipation more muted (Buehler & McFarland, 2001).

3. Recognize That Happiness Is Not Based on Circumstance

What it means: Whenever something tremendous or disastrous is predicted in a future scenario, we can take comfort in knowing that our contentment is not based on circumstances.

In many ways, happiness is relative. When we can remove unrealistic expectations, we can maintain a healthier perspective concerning the future. We should remind ourselves that our brains are programmed to regain homeostasis and find contentment regardless of outcomes.

What it looks like in practice:

Happiness is a choice, and it is up to us to choose it intentionally daily. The key is implementing practices that condition the mind to shift perspective from the negative to the positive.

1. Smile more consistently. Smiling lowers the release of the stress hormone cortisol and releases dopamine, endorphins, and serotonin in the brain (Cross et al., 2022).

2. Say daily affirmations to yourself. Self-affirmations promote increased activity in brain regions that produce self-perception: the medial prefrontal cortex, posterior cingulate cortex, and ventral striatum (Cascio et al., 2016). When activated, these systems are associated with improved self-image, future-oriented planning, and increased physical activity.

3. Reduce verbal complaints. Complaining is found to impact mood negatively. In addition, persistent complaining alters the brain's structures, increasing the risk of mood disorders and lowering the brain's capacity to maintain focus (Wojciszke et al., 2009).

Why it works: Wilson and Gilbert say that we have within our DNA a capacity to find contentment in the worst of circumstances (T. Wilson & Gilbert, 2005). When this knowledge is kept at the forefront of our minds, we can control impact bias.

CONCLUSION

When we overestimate the negative impact of change, it shatters our equilibrium, producing stress and anxiety. This reaction leads to a strong resistance to change. On an individual level, it will inhibit personal growth. On a professional level, it will reduce the ability to implement needed organizational change successfully. Although our tendency to overestimate the impact of change is pervasive, our conscious awareness of the behavior is low because it happens within 200 milliseconds, well before conscious thought. However, when educators and administrators are aware of impact bias, they can proactively engage in practices that prevent unintended consequences and help us achieve personal and professional change.

CHAPTER 5

....

YOU HAD ME AT HELLO

Face, Hands, Posture, Gesture, and Tone of Voice

CHAPTER OVERVIEW

▶ Neuroscience tells us that within 200 milliseconds of seeing anyone, our brains subconsciously reach many conclusions about that person. There are 1,000 milliseconds in one second. Anything that happens within 200 milliseconds is entirely subconscious. **Subconscious** means that it happens so fast that you are not aware, but since it has happened, it will influence your future thoughts and actions. This means that before you can consciously formulate an opinion about a person, your brain has already done it.

THE PREATTENTIONAL SYSTEM

We have a preattentional system that assesses the emotional expression of others in 140 to 200 milliseconds (Schyns et al., 2009). **Preattentional** means that it occurs subconsciously, influencing conscious thought at 500 milliseconds or later. Within 200 milliseconds, we have assessed emotions, predicted behavior, and been biased. This ability to predict behavior is a vital survival function. The process is efficient because it is one of the oldest brain processes, significantly preceding the inception of language. Although language is considered humans' most extraordinary and adaptive skill, it alone is insufficient for successful communication (Pinker, 1994). Interpreting emotions gives language its deeper meaning. Therefore, it is safe to say that emotional expression is the foundation of social communication and understanding. That means there is a correlation between higher empathy and proper language interpretation. People with low empathy often lose the nuance of emotional expressions that give meaning to language. The result is they become offended or angry by what was said due to a gross misinterpretation. One of the outcomes of low empathy is callousness toward the opinions of others due to a sense of overimportance. It is curious that the people who often voice vigorous offenses to what is being said are both prone to misinterpreting intent and insensitive to the feelings of others.

> *Emotional expression is the foundation of social communication and understanding.*

People read facial expressions so efficiently that they occur even at our periphery (Smith & Rossit, 2018). Researchers have found that our accuracy in interpreting facial expressions is just as precise when viewing people in profile as when viewing them from the front (Matsumoto & Hwang, 2011). Observing emotional expression produces empathy because the process triggers mirror neurons, which activate **motor neurons**, which imitate the behavior seen (T. Lee et al., 2008). The act of simulating the movements of others allows us to have a shared chemical experience with someone else.

Mirror Neurons

Mirror neurons are found in multiple brain areas, including the premotor cortex, supplementary motor area, primary somatosensory cortex, amygdala, thalamus, and inferior parietal cortex (Eysenck & Keane, 2015; Penagos-Corzo et al., 2022). In other words, it involves the parts of the brain involved with movement, senses, emotion, and awareness of where we are in relation to others. **Mirror neurons** play a role in initiating, planning, coordinating movements, and recording learned actions. Neuroscience shows that mirror neurons impact our ability to learn new skills and acquire emotional information from those around us (Cook et al., 2014). Imagine if your brain could not recognize or replicate movement patterns. A significant portion of brain function is dedicated to identifying, interpreting, and anticipating the movements of others. You see two people approaching each other, and from the look on their faces, you guess they are in love. You anticipate that they will embrace and then walk off arm in arm. The ability to recognize and predict behavior is a vital function of mirror neurons. Mirror neurons have us mimic behaviors in our minds as if we were doing it ourselves. If practice makes perfect, mirror neurons are vital to learning and improving any skill performed with the body (Acharya & Shukla, 2012; C. Wilson, 2014).

> *Mirror neurons impact our ability to learn new skills and acquire emotional information from those around us (Cook et al., 2014).*

Mirror neurons are strongly associated with empathy because when watching any expressive movement, we put ourselves in another's place (Penagos-Corzo et al., 2022). Researchers believe that we can understand the thoughts, emotions, and sensations of others by simulating them in our minds (Rasmussen & Bliss, 2014). When we are experiencing pain, the **anterior cingulate cortex** activates. A study showed that when we observe pain, the same region of the brain activates (Rasmussen & Bliss, 2014). However, the shared experience does not occur if mirror neurons are not activated. Interestingly, studies of individuals with autism spectrum disorder (ASD) have shown that individuals with ASD have dysfunctional mirror neurons, hindering some forms of social comprehension (Oberman & Ramachandran, 2007).

> *We can understand the thoughts, emotions, and sensations of others by simulating them in our minds (Rasmussen & Bliss, 2014).*

COMMUNICATION AND EMOTION

There are many theories that claim to explain how and why humans developed speech. The first established theory is that language started with people imitating the natural sounds around them, and eventually, they started using these sounds to talk to each other (Vaneechoutte & Skoyles, 1998). Those sounds turned into words over hundreds of thousands of years, and words were strung together significantly later. The other accepted theory, a more recent idea, is that people use emotional expressions, like gestures, postures, facial expressions, and sounds using different tones, to communicate (S. Gross, 2010). Eventually, these gestures became sign language and evolved into words coupled with emotional expressions. This is commonly referred to as the gesture-first theory of language.

Another debate involves when humans began to speak. One theory proposes that humans started speaking about 1.75 million years ago. This theory aligns the inception of language with stone toolmaking. Researchers have found that toolmaking and language share neural substrates, and hypotheses suggest that they emerged together (Uomini & Meyer, 2013). Another theory states that speech cannot precede the earliest date of the finding of the FOXP2 gene. The FOXP2 gene governs the embryonic development of the subcortical structures involved in speech and language. This is known to be the starting point for human speech about 50,000 years ago because it was absent in Neanderthals and earlier humans (Liberman, 2007).

Regardless of which theory of speech you adhere to, emotional expression precedes it. As a result, the assessment of emotions is viewed as a very early brain process, and language is a much later addition. When language was introduced, the emotional process accompanied it and continues today.

> *The assessment of emotions is viewed as a very early brain process, and language is a much later addition.*

Facial Expression

Although we are born with the ability to interpret facial expressions, the skill continues to develop over our lifespan. By age 1, infants can accurately identify major emotions (A. Gross & Ballif, 1991). Caregiver is sad, baby becomes sadder; caregiver is happy, baby becomes happier. Between the ages of 9 and 10, there is a significant improvement in our accuracy in identifying a wider range of emotions. An additional jump in accuracy occurs between 13 and 14 years of age, with the addition of the essential element of **response**

(Kolb et al., 1992). Empathy is supposed to produce an appropriate response in humans. If we see someone in distress, we are supposed to be motivated to respond appropriately. In many ways, identification without response is callous.

We should peak in emotional evaluation and response during ages 20 to 39. We experience a drop in the chemical response our brain generates to the emotions of others during the ages of 50 to 64 (Carstensen et al., 2000; Charles et al., 2001; Phillips et al., 2008). This lessens the effect that negative emotional expressions have on us. Some see this as the beginning of wisdom, lowering our emotions and increasing prefrontal cortex activation. A small percentage of people 65 and older lose the ability to detect threats (Charles & Pasupathi, 2003). This change might be the main reason older adults are targets of scams and may lose the ability to identify people with bad intentions, increasing gullibility.

The developmental ability to interpret facial expressions assumes that you have engaged in an appropriate amount of face-to-face interactions and emotional assessment at various ages. One often-discussed issue is that the drop in empathy is linked to the increased use of technology as a primary means of communication. Modern communication methods, such as texting, emails, and social media, tend to impede empathic cues from our interactions (Riess, 2017). Although we are born with the capacity to have empathy, both quality and quantity of emotional interactions throughout our lifespan are required to become an efficient brain process.

> *The drop in empathy is linked to the increased use of technology as a primary means of communication.*

However, other forms of technology have been found effective for eliciting and teaching empathy. A study measured empathy response and social bonding and found significant differences based on the method of interaction. The most significant empathy and bonding occurred during in-person interaction. Video chat was next, audio chat was a close third, and instant messaging was the least effective (Sherman et al., 2013). A promising technology for teaching social behavior and improving empathy response has been virtual reality. Virtual reality has been identified as one of the most promising resources for developing a better social understanding of behavior and eliciting empathy responses from individuals with low empathy (Marques et al., 2022). This technology might provide schools with a method for training empathy in a nonthreatening approach.

Gestures

Our preattentional system also focuses on hand gestures. Some scientists conjecture that this focus could have evolved from gestures being the first language medium (Wallman, 1992). Studies suggest that the link between hand gestures and language still exists today. Very young children demonstrate increased language acquisition when speech is coupled with gestures (Ramos-Cabo et al., 2019). Recent neuroscience experiments tested the gesture-first theory of language origin, and their findings support this theory. They found that gestures were more universally understood within cultures, across cultures, and even for participants who are severely vision-impaired (despite the absence of a shared visual experience) (Fay et al., 2022).

> *Children demonstrate increased language acquisition when speech is coupled with gestures (Ramos-Cabo et al., 2019).*

Our early attention system monitors hand gestures, indicating subconscious awareness between 150 to 200 milliseconds, followed by conscious awareness around 600 milliseconds

(Flaisch et al., 2009; Flaisch et al., 2011). However, the chemical impact of all gestures is not equal. We are alerted more quickly to negative gestures, and their effect is more substantial on the brain when compared to positive gestures. Neutral gestures receive the lowest activation, positive ones receive higher activation, and negative ones receive the highest activation. The subconscious activation level is predictive of the intensity of our response when we become conscious of the gestures. This is why things perceived as negative garner the most potent response: Our chemical reaction at a subconscious level has primed our mind and body on how to respond.

Posture

Emotion can be communicated in many ways. An often-ignored modality is posture. We can usually distinguish emotions such as joy, sadness, fear, anger, and disgust at a glance merely by seeing someone's posture. A recent study revealed that individuals accurately categorized posture (Lopez et al., 2017). Participants were able to identify not only the category of emotion but also the level of intensity. Additional studies have shown that people can detect even relatively small differences in body posture and movement influencing emotion perception (Dael et al., 2012).

Our brains are wired to monitor a range of emotional cues in milliseconds to improve accuracy and understanding. A study found that participants rated facial expressions more accurately when seeing someone's body posture. Not only was accuracy improved, but a greater empathic response was also experienced (Treal et al., 2021). This finding is significant because the empathy response occurred in a virtual world experiment. The finding shows that the empathy response is so hardwired that people experience it even when they know the lifelike figure is not human and cannot feel the emotions displayed.

Research has determined that the impact of an outward emotion on the brain can be inversed. Usually, the brain has to mirror emotions to experience the chemical impact. However, when researchers had people take on a posture externally, it influenced their mood. For example, having participants demonstrate an upright sitting posture increased positive mood states and the brain's processing speed (Awad et al., 2021). The findings imply that posture manipulation may affect cognitive performance and mood. The implications here cannot be overstated; we are in greater control of our moods and cognitive state than ever imagined.

> *Posture manipulation may affect cognitive performance and mood.*

Teachers should be aware of how their body posture influences students and how they can be influenced. A study found that patients who viewed their physicians as displaying empathic nonverbal behavior viewed them as more competent (Kraft-Todd et al., 2017). However, not only were physicians viewed as unempathetic seen as less competent, but patients became less communicative as well, negatively impacting their care. The conclusion was that what we do with our bodies to communicate empathy has real-world ramifications. In the medical field, it impacts patients' options toward their physician and their emotional and physical health. The implications for education are not less significant. What teachers communicate with their bodies affects how students view and respond. The converse should also be considered: What students project with their bodies also impacts the quality of teacher performance. Therefore, there is a need for teachers to explain how the body impacts mood and cognitive performance and to reach some agreement with students on how both should purport themselves to maximize performance.

Mirroring is the subconscious replication of another person's posture and expressions. Automatic mimicry plays a role in both empathy and attraction. We began mirroring people we were drawn to as infants; a parent made a facial expression, and we attempted to return the same expression. The natural tendency to mirror someone's body posture is a precursor to healthy social development (Prochazkova & Kret, 2017). People with certain social disorders such as autism, sociopathy, or psychopathy do not naturally engage in mirroring. Individuals on the autism spectrum possess neurological complications that impact cognitive functioning, sensory processing, motor skills, speech, information processing, and social skills, which affect how people interact with others. *Sociopathy* is the umbrella term used to refer to individuals who display a pattern of antisocial behaviors, including manipulation, deceit, and aggression, that stem from a lack of empathy for others. *Psychopathy* describes a condition characterized by the absence of empathy, which produces a callousness toward the emotions of others, which can create a range of manipulative and sadistic behaviors. These social disorders share some level of impairment to the mirror neuron system.

Mirroring someone's body language shows a stronger connection between two people or a desire to bond. It is considered a more intense response because it is not only mirror neurons activating in the brain but also an external expression of empathy. When the two individuals in social situations display similar nonverbal gestures, they take on a mental synergy that causes subconscious rapport. Mimicry can become contagious (Feldman et al., 2011). When a group of socially connected people are together, one body movement can have a ripple effect across the group. People are generally not consciously aware of how frequently they shift their bodies to mirror the movements of others daily (Dimberg et al., 2000; Tamietto & de Gelder, 2010; Wood et al., 2016).

Mirroring can be an effective strategy used by educators to build rapport with students.

Teachers who mirrored their students reported significantly higher perceptions of rapport, more confidence in learning outcomes, and significantly higher quiz scores. The study compared teachers using imitation as a teaching strategy to build teacher–student relationships and found that they outperformed teachers in the control group who did not mirror students (Zhou, 2012). School administrators should also employ the strategy because it has been found to improve rapport and work performance in staff (Dimberg et al., 2000).

> *Teachers who mirrored their students reported significantly higher perceptions of rapport, more confidence in learning outcomes, and significantly higher quiz scores.*

Voice and Tone

When we hear someone speak, our brains assess **vocal stimuli** first to determine emotions. Within 150 to 200 milliseconds, we determine positive and negative emotional vocalizations (Fecteau et al., 2007). The assessment of emotions biases how we interpret the words. Immediately after assessing for emotions, our brain engages in an **identity match**. By 300 milliseconds, we have made many assessments concerning the person talking (gender, age, health, race, etc.) (Roswandowitz et al., 2018). It is not until around 600 milliseconds that we begin to process words (Spreckelmeyer et al., 2009). Since word recognition occurs after emotion and identifiers have already biased us, we can conclude that the meaning of language is not a simple process of understanding words based on definition, order, and context. A 2018 study had participants stress the tone of specific words in the sentence, "I never said she stole my money." Researchers found that it changed in meaning based on which word was emphasized (Dichter et al., 2018). Not only did tone change the meaning in several ways, but it also determined if the words were a sentence or a question.

The ability to assess emotion and conduct identity matches has evolved so much that we can do it accurately after hearing one word (Baus et al., 2019). The researchers had participants say only one word—*hello*. Participants could accurately determine the speaker's emotional state and evaluate personality traits from that one word. One of the most impressive findings is that researchers found that we could understand emotions and who was talking even when the word said was by a foreign speaker in a different language. These results prove that our ability to assess voice tone to determine emotion and identifiers is accurate across cultures and languages.

> *Our ability to assess voice tone to determine emotion and identifiers is accurate across cultures and languages.*

Stranger Danger

The brain might also use different processes when we hear a familiar voice versus the voice of a stranger. Numerous neural studies show a slightly different neural pathway for identifying familiar versus unfamiliar voices. When we hear a familiar voice, a network involving most regions in the **temporal lobe,** some regions in the **frontal lobe, subcortical structures,** and areas around the **marginal lobes** are activated. The bilateral superior temporal gyrus is also recruited when we hear an unfamiliar voice (Sun et al., 2023). The **bilateral superior temporal gyrus** helps us gain a social perception when processing language (Jou et al., 2010), which may involve determining whether someone is a friend or foe. The bilateral superior temporal gyrus can make this determination completely absent of linguistic content (Rupp et al., 2022). Recognizing the voice tone of who you know instantaneously alters emotional behaviors and is essential to survival and a sense of belonging to a clan. Interestingly, the superior temporal gyrus, implicated in language processing and social perception, is a consistent anatomical abnormality in children and adolescents with autism (Jou et al., 2010). The finding supports that tone analysis plays a significant role in determining social perception.

> *Recognizing the voice tone of who you know instantaneously alters emotional behaviors and is essential to survival and a sense of belonging.*

How we process speech has a wide range of implications for teachers. Whenever emotion is perceived when a student speaks, it will bias the interpretation of language positively or negatively. How we feel about the student's talking matters because emotion will always determine who is talking. Therefore, teachers are likely to have favorable interpretations of what is being said by students who are upbeat and liked. However, there are less favorable interpretations of what is being said by students who project negative emotions and are less likable. The likely outcome is that we miss profound statements made by students who are not perceived as "good students." Missing the opportunity to reinforce the positive contributions of struggling students is more significant than teachers might know. When we reinforce the performance of struggling students, they experience success, which triggers the hormone we associate with motivation. The ability to nurture a sequence of success can motivate the unmotivated student.

RESILIENCE AND GRIT

A recent adage that has grown in popularity is that unmotivated students lack "grit." The appropriate recourse is to stop coddling them and demand performance—"or else." **Grit** is defined as firmness of mind or spirit, unyielding courage, and the ability to grind on. This sounds logical based on a casual observation of student behavior, but is not supported by science. Another word for grit is **resiliency**, the ability to bounce back from difficult circumstances and achieve success. An infant is not born gritty or resilient. Neuroscience found that safe and predictable environments help the brain and body develop a healthy stress response system. The stress response system is called the **hypothalamic-pituitary-adrenocortical (HPA) axis** (Sheng et al., 2021). It is comprised of the hypothalamus, the pituitary gland, and the adrenal cortex and regulates hormones, particularly the stress hormone cortisol. This system can rapidly increase glucose levels, speed the heart rate, and increase blood flow to the muscles to allow an immediate response to threats. The other factor determining the healthy development of an infant's HPA axis is receiving positive nonverbal emotional cues. When frequently exposed to danger or experiencing trauma, the HPA axis can experience an adaptation to inhibit the ability to regulate stress and regain equilibrium (McEwen, 2017). It is clear that the ability of our brain and body to cope with stress is born out of not confrontation and demand but safety and nurturance.

Later in life, our resilience is born out of a pattern of success. **Motivation** is a product of success frequency, which triggers a sequence of **molecules** (peptides, hormones, and neurotransmitters) that produce what is commonly known as **intrinsic motivation** (van der Kooij et al., 2021). Watch what any average student does when doing their homework assignments. Logic dictates that they attend to their worst subjects first because they need more time and focus. However, that is different from what usually happens: They first attend to the subjects in which they excel because of their pattern of success, which produces chemical motivation. Consider the struggling student who has yet to achieve a pattern of academic success. He is unmotivated; if he tries, one setback is often enough to get him to quit. In neuroscience, grit is achieving a pattern of success in an area that produces confidence, so much so that a few setbacks are not enough to extinguish internal motivation. Therefore, students need to maintain a pattern of success to be resilient. Another way to think about resiliency is to consider video game design. If a game is too easy and you always win, you will quit because it gives you no sense of accomplishment. If the game is too hard and you fail all the time, you will quit playing; no chemical motivation is provided by success. The best video game allows you to win more at the beginning, triggering motivation, and at each ascending level makes it more challenging so that you improve your skills while success is still attainable.

> **Students need to maintain a pattern of success to be resilient.**

Achieving the correct formula to promote student motivation is challenging. Teachers instruct students with diverse skill levels, and finding the correct level of challenge for each is difficult. Using emotional cues allows teachers to improve their communication accuracy with students from diverse cognitive and cultural backgrounds. Empathy with good differentiated instructional strategies provides a good foundation for helping all students achieve a pattern of success.

INNER SPEECH

One might wonder why a section on tonality would include inner speech. Inner speech is an internalized dialogue without audible sound, also known as the voice inside your head. When we participate in inner speech, we engage the exact mechanisms of outer speech (Whitford et al., 2017). **Numerous electroencephalographic (EEG)** and **magnetoencephalographic (MEG)** studies have found that motor neurons activate as if we engage in outer speech when we do inner speech. Surprisingly, our auditory processing activates as if we are hearing the words. Most surprisingly, if the inner speech carries an emotional message, it activates the appropriate chemical responses. Consider students who suffer from depression. It is widely known that people with clinically diagnosed depression tend to ruminate on their problems and repeat negative messages to themselves. Imagine the chemical impact of such a practice. Each time the person with depression engages in negative inner speech, they compound the negative chemical impact on their brains. The chemical impact is reflected in their thought and actions.

Teachers should focus on teaching students to engage in affirming inner speech. This simple action could improve their brain chemistry, perceptions of the world, and sense of empowerment.

RECOMMENDATIONS FOR EDUCATORS

1. Use Gestures to Reduce Cognitive Load

What it is: Gesturing supports language processing and has been found to reduce cognitive load and improve working memory (Marstaller & Burianová, 2013). When students reach cognitive load, they require a brief recovery period during which their brains are not entirely focused. Consider the English learners in your classroom; they are attempting not only to grasp new information, but also to understand the content: Their brains have to translate every word. Research has found translating a new language to be mentally exhausting. The result is that they hit their limit of cognitive load faster. Once their brains regain the ability to focus, so much information has been said that they often cannot comprehend what the teacher is saying.

What it looks like in practice: Teachers can utilize gestures to reduce cognitive load in the following ways:

- **Universal expressive gestures,** which help all students comprehend language faster. Teachers who are excited about the information they are presenting tend to gesture more.

- **Formal gestures,** which teachers use to cue certain information. For example, a teacher might use a gesture corresponding to a learning section. Every day during that section, the teacher begins with that gesture.

  Another example is a gesture used for specific information, like a key vocabulary word. Every time the word is said, the corresponding gesture is made. For example, the teacher introduces the word *amygdala* and shows a picture that illustrates that it looks like the shape of an almond. The teacher has the students make an almond shape by touching the thumb to the index finger while repeating the word *amygdala*. Each time the word is said in the future, the teacher will model the gesture and have students follow it.

  Gestures can also cue an action, like a gesture to denote when it is time to line up. For example, each time the teacher says it is time to line up, she wiggles her index and middle fingers, making a walking gesture. Over time, the teacher needs only to make the gesture to cue the behavior.

Why it works: Gestures improve focus, recall, and compliance. Gestures are even more effective when teachers can get students to mimic the gestures. Teachers who have established a good rapport with their students reduce cognitive load. When we have rapport, empathy is increased. The higher the empathy, the more effective gestures are in conveying meaning in language (Chu & Hagoort, 2014). Because we tend to mirror people we have a rapport with, we learn their repeated gestures, and those movements carry meaning. As a result, students who struggle with language do better with teachers with whom they have a good rapport.

2. Emotional Control

What it is: Many social-emotional learning curriculums over-complicate the concept of emotional control. The human brain is transformed by what we do consistently. Therefore, specific actions have been proven to promote positive brain chemistry, improving cognitive performance, emotional disposition, and social behavior. Earlier, it was established that there is a direct correlation between the body and brain chemistry. For example, what we feel is often expressed on our faces, and what we do with our faces can influence our moods.

What it looks like in practice: One of the most powerful lessons we can teach children is how to utilize their bodies to maximize their chemical disposition for success.

- Teach students to adopt smiling. Smiling influences the social states of others through mirror neurons, improving student interactions.

- Encourage good sitting posture. Figure 5.1 shows an example of what good sitting posture looks like compared to bad sitting posture. Teachers can use diagrams like this in the classroom to serve as visual reminders to students.

FIGURE 5.1   INCORRECT (LEFT) VS. CORRECT (RIGHT) SITTING POSTURE

SOURCE: istock.com/Ladadik Art

Why it works: Neuroimaging studies show that seeing and expressing a smile engages the orbitofrontal cortex with the amygdala and hippocampus (Stark et al., 2020). Smiling involves cognition, emotion, and memory. Research also shows that manipulating a smile improves memory performance (Kuehne et al., 2021). Smiling changes the social climate of the classroom.

Posture stimulates the brain's awareness and attention systems, positively influencing cognition and memory (Muehlhan et al., 2014).

3. Adopting Affirming Inner Speech

What it is: We have learned that inner speech can alter the brain's chemistry based on the emotions expressed in the message. However, it is strongly recommended not to stop at instruction alone. The key to influencing behavior is practice. Repeated practice increases the importance of the brain prioritizing the action. Also, repeated practice lowers the energy required to do the behavior, increasing the likelihood it will occur.

What it looks like in practice:

- Teach students about the impact that inner speech has on their moods.

- Begin the class by having students repeat three affirming phases out loud. Once they have practiced saying the phrases regularly, reteach the lesson on inner speech. Examples of affirming phrases include the following:

- *I can do hard things.*

- *I believe in myself.*

- *I am capable of achieving my goals.*

- *I will do my best at everything I attempt.*

- *I choose to be in a good mood.*

- *I choose to have a positive attitude.*

- *I make the best of every situation.*

- *I have control over my thoughts and feelings.*

- *I treat others with respect.*

- *I choose to smile no matter how I feel.*

- *I am a capable student.*

- *I can do difficult things.*

- *I can take on challenges and become more resilient.*

- *My hard work will pay off.*

- *Today, I will do my best.*

- *I am brave and strong.*

- *I can do anything I set my mind to.*

- *I am unique and special.*

- *I am kind and honest.*

- *I am a good friend.*
- *I have many talents and abilities.*
- *I am smart and capable.*
- *I can handle challenges with determination.*
- *I am creative and imaginative.*
- *I can learn anything I want to learn.*
- *I am confident.*
- *I am a good listener and helper.*
- *I am always improving and growing.*
- *I am a good role model for other students.*
- *I will have a positive influence on those around me.*
- *I am a great friend and make others feel valued.*
- *I am an important part of my classroom community.*
- *I am responsible and dependable.*
- *I am a good at play.*
- *I am a lifelong learner.*

Why it works: When a behavior is routinely done, dopamine is more likely to reinforce it, creating a long-term habit. Having three phrases they can say to themselves whenever they feel that other people have made them question their self-worth will be a tool students can use anytime.

CONCLUSION

So much of the social interaction between teachers, between students, and between students and teachers is influenced by what our brain perceives in the first 200 milliseconds of every interaction. The evolution of language has caused us to believe that communication is primarily based on what we say. However, we are reminded daily that facial expressions, gestures, postures, and voice tone highly influence how we interpret language during social interaction. Teachers who become aware of the preattentional systems become mindful of what the subconscious brain focuses on during social interactions and can better influence social and academic outcomes positively. Also, being more intentional in monitoring students' faces, hands, postures, gestures, and voice tones will improve classroom management. Early alertness to students' emotional conditions can enable teachers to check in on students who seem to be in trouble, or defuse tensions between students before they lead to incidents. One study found a strong correlation between teachers' effective use of nonverbal communication and student outcomes in academic performance and social behavior (Bambaeeroo & Shokrpour, 2017).

CHAPTER 6

....

PATTERN BEHAVIOR

Patterns in Our Environment Create Bias

CHAPTER OVERVIEW

▶ Disproportionate patterns in the school environment produce implicit bias, which can adversely affect the behaviors of even the most supportive teachers. Educators should learn to identify negative patterns in the school climate that can produce implicit biases, and seek to alter the patterns.

OUR BRAIN LOOKS FOR PATTERNS

Implicit bias occurs because the brain looks for patterns and makes associations in order to learn. **Social cognition,** the ability to store, process, and apply information about people in social situations, depends on this ability to make associations in day-to-day life. Once a pattern has been observed consistently and associations have been made, the brain establishes shortcuts to improve efficiency.

It is important to remember the distinction between associations that operate mostly unconsciously, producing **implicit biases,** and those that are intentional and controllable, known as **explicit biases.** While explicit biases are within our control, implicit biases often go unchallenged due to a lack of awareness.

> *While explicit biases are within our control, implicit biases often go unchallenged due to a lack of awareness.*

A person can explicitly disapprove of a certain attitude or belief while still possessing contradictory biases on an unconscious level. These biases, which are a universal part of human cognition, do not align with our sense of self and personal identity. Because we understand ourselves based on conscious thoughts, we tend not to think we are susceptible to biases. The reality is that everyone automatically develops biases because of how the brain learns and attempts to make sense of the world. Most implicit biases have little to do with individuals' inclination to discriminate against others. It is the brain at work making associations and generalizations of which we are unaware.

Our brains' tendency to look for patterns, make associations, and take shortcuts guarantees that daily environments will produce some biases. Although societal conditioning and personal experiences contribute to implicit associations, most environments will produce some biases independently.

DISPROPORTIONATE PATTERNS DEVELOP BIASES

Specific disproportionate patterns in education are so pervasive that they are consistently seen in schools that serve certain student groups (Breese et al., 2023). One of these pervasive patterns is commonly referred to as the positive bias. Results indicate that teachers display a significant positive bias toward Asian students relative to white students regarding academic performance (Shi & Zhu, 2023). An educational longitudinal study found that teachers have three expectations of Asian students: higher attentiveness and performance in the classroom, greater future educational attainment, and the need to make recommendations for Advanced Placement (AP) and Honors courses (Okura, 2022). The latter expectation illustrates how biases have immediate and long-term implications. Asian students getting more AP and Honors course referrals directly correlates to advantages in college opportunities and career pathways. This bias has become so well accepted that some scholars have gone as far as to contend that differences in tested cognitive ability of Asian students are rooted in genetics (Herrnstein & Murray, 1994). The root of the Asian bias in education has not been identified; however, what is not in dispute is that it is evident in schools that have an Asian student population.

Another disproportionate pattern in education is that English learners (ELs) will struggle academically. Currently, the negative view of second-language learners focuses on those who speak Spanish. The bias toward ELs is so closely tied to poor academic performance that being classified as a second-language learner in the first grade is predictive of negative scores in math and English through the tenth grade (Umansky, 2016). This implicit bias has led to a high number of ELs being misidentified as students with learning disabilities and thus placed into special education. A study found that teachers' low academic expectations were evident in body language, voice intonations, and facial expressions (İnan-Kaya & Rubie-Davies, 2022). The researcher concluded that teachers' implicit biases toward second-language learners were conveyed to students, negatively impacting academic performance. This conclusion was reached because teachers who did not convey negative nonverbal signals to students demonstrated better academic outcomes with the population.

Perhaps the most consistently seen disproportionate pattern in education is the assumption of poor academic and behavioral performance of Black male students. From the initial introduction to the educational system, Black males face low expectations that alter their academic trajectory (Gaylord-Harden et al., 2018). Early low expectations have long-term implications; teacher expectations in kindergarten predict academic achievement through secondary education (Hamre & Pianta, 2001). It has been proposed that the expectation of poor behavior detracts from academic expectations and the ability to forge meaningful relationships with Black male students. Early teacher–student relationships predict academic achievement through the eighth grade (Hu et al., 2021).

Laboratory experiments found that teachers rate the behaviors of Black males as more severe regardless of infraction and consistently administer more punitive disciplinary actions when compared to white males (Okonofua & Eberhardt, 2015). School records show that the length of suspensions assigned to Black versus white students was longer when they fought with each other (Barrett et al., 2017). This finding clearly illustrates how the same behavior is viewed and treated differently based on held implicit biases. Close observation of classroom teacher–student interactions consistently found that nonverbal attitudes toward Black males were less favorable than nonverbal attitudes toward white males (Ferguson, 2001). The most blatant indication of behavioral bias is that Black students made up only 16% of students in the United States but accounted for 42% of suspensions (Quereshi & Okonofua, 2017). Black male students are three times more likely than white male students to be suspended or expelled from school. Once a Black student is suspended, they are more likely to be suspended again (Quereshi & Okonofua, 2017).

CASE STUDY OF DISPROPORTIONATE PATTERNS IN A SCHOOL SETTING

Disproportionate patterns in education often become widespread because the educational design lacks variance. A disproportionate pattern occurs repeatedly in schools independently, and then the pattern becomes widely recognized and accepted. The patterns slowly create an unrecognized implicit bias, although the outcomes become pervasive. Educators accept the patterns and often make efforts to address them without knowing how much subconscious human behavior is contributing to the outcome. It is crucial to recognize that disproportionate patterns alter the educational experiences of teachers and students. A case study is provided to illustrate how the patterns mentioned earlier influence the educational experience on the ground. The following information is taken from a school climate assessment conducted by Resiliency Inc. The goal of the assessment was to provide a realistic example of how environmental patterns can produce biases. The name of the high school in the climate assessment has been changed.

Centurion High School has over 3,000 students and over 150 staff members. The student population is 74% white, 13% Asian, and 13% Black. The high school is known for its strong academics, music, and sports programs. It has produced several merit scholars and athletic championships. It is a large high school, with the building's circumference equaling a mile. As a result, Centurion High School has 17 full-time hall monitors who walk around with walkie-talkies and run to the locations of incidents in the hallways. The hall monitors are primarily physically fit young males. Teachers at the high school ignore incidents taking place in the hallways, believing that it is neither part of their job description nor in their contract.

During the assessment process, students were interviewed and asked a list of questions. Their responses were recorded and reported aggregately. One question asked was whether there are good students and bad students at Centurion High School. If the students responded yes, they were asked what a good student looks like. In schools with no bias related to the performance of any subset of students, the response to this question is, usually, like any of us. However, at Centurion High School, 83% of the students said that a good student looks Asian. The students even had a term for it. They called it "the Asian Factor." Students said that they perceived that most of the teachers at Centurion High School assumed that all Asian students are good at science, math, and music and are well behaved. These biases were based on a few well-established disproportionate patterns in the school environment. Although Asian students only represented 13% of the student population, they were disproportionately represented in Honors math classes, Honors science classes, and the school music program and not represented in student discipline records over a 10-year period. The pattern was so consistent that whenever we saw a classroom with a high concentration of Asian students, we would guess that it was an Honors class, and when we checked, the assumption was correct.

I personally interviewed an Asian student at Centurion High School, and when I asked him what a good student looks like, he said, "Haven't you heard about the Asian Factor?" I said, "No—explain it to me." He said that teachers at Centurion High School assume that every Asian student is good at science and math, musically inclined, and well behaved. He then told me about his freshman year in math at Centurion High School. He said that when he walked into his freshman math class, the teacher saw him and immediately said, "You will do great in this class." He promptly looked at her and said, "Lady, I am not one of those Asians." He then said that he failed his first quiz, and as she gave him his test back, he looked at her and said, "I told you, I am not one of those Asians." While leaving the class, she asked him what lunch period he had; when he told her, she said that it coincided with her planning period and asked if he could leave lunch 10 minutes early for a few days and come to her classroom. He said she proceeded to tutor him one-on-one for the next few weeks. I asked him how he did in the class; he said, "I got an A minus; she wouldn't let me fail."

Biases are not always negative or bad. Studies consistently show that positive attitudes influence brain chemistry and outcomes. Teachers who believe that all students will be successful have more successful student outcomes. Patients who believe they will overcome a disease or recover from surgery show better outcomes than those who do not. That is not to say that biases in and of themselves will predict outcomes. The reality is that biases motivate actions that influence outcomes. The teacher who believed that Asian students would succeed in math influenced the outcome through her actions. Some more cynical individuals would say the student already possessed the potential to do the math. That might be true, but that student did not believe he could excel in math. It was her belief in him that gave him the confidence and her actions that taught him the skills needed to be successful. The sad truth is that negative biases influence desired outcomes more than positive ones. The simple explanation could be that accepting and acting on a negative viewpoint is easier since we are predisposed to a negative bias. However, the truth is far more complex, and implicit negative bias is first conveyed through our face, hands, posture, gestures, and tone of voice. It is further supported by subtle actions made consciously and subconsciously. It can become overwhelming when others share the bias, and the onslaught of subconscious and conscious messages begins to shape a person's reality.

Students at Centurion High School were also asked if there were bad students. If they answered yes, they were asked what these students looked like. Over 90% of the students identified Black males. The students claimed that the adults at Centurion High School assumed that Black males struggle academically and are likely to have behavior problems. Students consistently reported that whenever an incident was reported in the hallways, if the hall monitors saw a Black male near the reported location, they would approach that male first, assuming he was involved. Black kids represented only 13% of the student body, with Black males between 4% and 6%, depending on the school year. However, this small fraction of the student population consistently represented 66% of students receiving special education services, 45% to 66% of the discipline data, and 60% to 80% of remedial classroom assignments. A 10-year review of discipline data found that Black males never comprised fewer than 46% of suspensions.

Because Centurion High School has a history of high academic standards, incoming freshmen who begin to struggle in core English and math classes are quickly referred to the remedial classes designed to help them catch up. Black males consistently comprised a high percentage of remedial classroom referrals. During the assessment, if we passed a classroom with a high concentration of Black male students, we could assume it was a remedial class, and when we checked, it was correct. Understand how patterns influence the brain. Black males at Centurion High School were consistently linked to behavioral incidents and suspensions, special education classes, and remedial programs. After exposure to the pattern, an individual at Centurion High School would see a Black male student and subconsciously associate him with behavioral issues and poor academic performance.

Bias Influences Perceptions and Outcomes

While conducting the school climate assessment, an incident occurred with the son of a Black female teacher at the school. A fight was reported in a hall between a group of Black males from a certain neighborhood in town. During the incident, her son was passing, and the hall monitors grabbed him, believing he was involved. Student onlookers reported to the monitors that he was not involved, but they ignored these statements. The teacher's son was suspended, and she appealed the suspension. After her son had served the suspension, missed classes, and lost the ability to participate in a football game, the review board determined that he was suspended in error. Surprisingly, the teacher's son was an Honors student, had never been in trouble, and was a star athlete. His mother reported that before the incident, her son was not focused on race and was happy and charismatic. Post-incident, he became very race-conscious and, at times, angry and moody.

This example illustrates that unconscious biases have casualties. Unintended actions can have life-altering ramifications. Wouldn't it be amazing if our biases all improved student outcomes, like the Asian Factor? However, too many incidents of implicit bias leave students scared and changed, like our Honors student-athlete at Centurion High School.

RECOMMENDATIONS FOR EDUCATORS

1. **Notice Patterns**

What it is: Educators should actively look for patterns in the school environment that can produce negative biases. Many times, simple rational decisions produce unintended biases. We decide to put our struggling readers in their own small reading group and fail to see that they are all English learners. We religiously review school performance data and are unaware that the repeated association of a small subgroup of students with poor performance subconsciously associates them with academic failure. Decisions that can produce sub-conscious biases are often born not out of malicious intent, but rather out of practicality or caring. That is the nature of implicit bias: It is there, unnoticed, and over time it can become part of the institution's fabric. In everyone's defense, the brain cannot attend to what it is unaware of.

2. Change What People See

What it is: If patterns produce bias, the simple answer is to change the pattern. Too many schools approach the issue of implicit bias by attempting to get people to admit that they are biased. The logic seems flawed. If implicit bias is a sub-conscious process, one is unaware. Therefore, looking for patterns that can produce a bias and changing the pattern is a productive exercise that most educators can agree with. For example, Centurion High School ended remedial classes. However, they did not return students to English and math classes without support. The remedial classroom teachers provided full-time support in these classes, offering one-on-one assistance to students who needed it. In addition, any student failing English or math was required to attend after-school support. Also, students who excel in English or math were invited to provide tutorial support for extra credit. The same after-school support rooms were used by student-athletes as their study space before and after practices. The mixture of students ensured that when you looked at the students in the after-school support program, you saw a wide representation of the student population.

In addition, a schoolwide social skills program was instituted that focused on increasing social interactions between students from different backgrounds. Also, a student mentorship program was established, in which seniors were each assigned a freshman to mentor. The mentor was to check in with the freshman at least once a week. The program was kicked off with a field trip in which the seniors and freshmen were introduced and had to go through a skills competition in which they were assigned tasks to complete that required them to work together. These two initiatives reduced social conflicts at the school and improved the overall school climate. The proactive approach to improve the social climate positively impacted the discipline data of Black male students.

3. **Balance Data**

What it is: One unexpected outcome of the consistent performance data review is that underperforming subgroups become associated with failure. The pattern quickly creates implicit bias. One alternative is to include change data in the academic performance review process. Change data chart how much progress a student has made. The result is that teachers notice the effort and growth capacity of students who may not be working on grade level but are making progress. The charting of change data was reported by teachers as a revelation. They began to notice more significant gains made by struggling students, and that reframed their thinking about the students' efforts. Viewing students differently positively impacts nonverbal cues. The change in nonverbal cues improves teacher–student relationships and conveys greater confidence in the students.

4. **Have an Empathic Response to Casualties of Bias**

What it is: School administrators might want to adopt a process to determine whether a discipline incident is or could be influenced by implicit bias. If the review process determines that implicit bias might play a role, they follow a simple three-step process.

What it looks like:

- Step 1: Explain

  Explain why the mistake was made. This is an honest explanation of how the pattern is identified. The identification of the pattern helps explain why the association is easily made.

- Step 2: Empathize

  Allow the student to express how they felt and truly empathize with them. Empathy, in this case, is defined as mirroring the student's emotional expressions coupled with an apology. Mirroring helps operationalize the empathy process. Plus, mirroring helps people build trust.

- Step 3: Correct

  Explain to the students the corrective measures that will be implemented in hopes of the mistake not being repeated.

5. **Checks and Balances for Suspensions**

The research mentioned earlier on student discipline illustrates how administrators unwittingly assign harsher consequences to Black male students. Some simple strategies help school leaders not fall into the pattern of administering more punitive consequences to Black male students.

What it looks like:

1. Conduct a brief review of consequences administered to other students for similar factors and determine to make the discipline equal to those.

2. Have another administrator review the incident without identifying the student and make a disciplinary recommendation.

These two strategies help administrators recognize the tendency to consider harsher consequences for disciplinary infractions against Black males. That realization often makes school leaders cognizant of the implicit pattern. Sensitivity to the issue can help school leaders avoid disproportionate responses in the future.

CONCLUSION

Disproportionate patterns in education are so consistent that they become expected and difficult to break. These patterns often influence how students view education from the first point of contact, altering the trajectory of their educational futures. However, these patterns can be addressed if we change what people see. We can create another approach that eliminates negative patterns while addressing presenting problems. In addition, educators should establish protocols and systems that break the negative outcome of established patterns in the school environments. The good news is that most educators would be saddened by the devastating outcome that many disproportionate patterns produce. Once they become aware, they will be motivated to change the patterns.

CHAPTER 7

....

CULTURE CLUB
How Culture Can Shape Bias

CHAPTER OVERVIEW

▶ The emergence of cultural neuroscience has proven that environmental factors can dramatically change gene expression. As a result, culture alters how the brain views the self, others, and the world. However, awareness of how culture transforms the brain can help educators become more accepting of the difference in approach and perspective caused by culture.

WHAT DO PEOPLE MEAN WHEN THEY SAY "CULTURE"?

It should be stated that conversations about culture in America are extremely confusing. The traditional definition of **culture** is the characteristics and knowledge of a particular group of people, encompassing language, religion, cuisine, social habits, music, and arts. Are people referring to the classic definition of the word when they say "culture"?

Neuroscience has proven that **neural plasticity** and **epigenesis**—the development of a plant or animal from an egg or spore through a series of processes in which unorganized cell masses differentiate into organs and organ systems—demonstrate that significant experiences alter brain development in nongenetic ways. As a result, environmental factors can dramatically change gene expression (Gunnar et al., 2001; T. I. Lee et al., 2006; Meaney & Syzf, 2005; Suomi et al., 1999). This has given birth to a field called cultural neuroscience. **Cultural neuroscience** examines how specific tools, practices, and tasks foster brain changes and bias how the brain performs tasks.

One of the areas that cultural neuroscience has focused on during its infancy is the differences between individualist and collectivist cultures. The core difference between these cultures is how people view themselves in relation to others. A **collectivist culture** places group concerns above those of the individual (Triandis, 2018). In an **individualist culture**, the concerns of the individual are placed above those of the group (Oyserman et al., 2002). Cultural neuroscience began here because it has such a rich data pool. Individualist nations include the United States, the United Kingdom, Canada, Germany, the Netherlands, Switzerland, South Africa, Ireland, Finland, Australia, Hungary (post-communist generation), and New Zealand (Načinović Braje et al., 2019). Collectivist cultures include China, India, Pakistan, Japan, Bangladesh, Indonesia, Egypt, Korea, Lebanon, Afghanistan, Saudi Arabia, Russia, and Kenya (Načinović Braje et al., 2019).

CULTURE CAN INFLUENCE HOW WE VIEW THE WORLD

A well-developed body of research indicates that individualist and collectivist cultures view the world slightly differently because of how they view themselves. The altered view is evident in attention, contextual processing, categorization, and reasoning. As a result, in a 2001 study, researchers used eye-tracking technology to analyze how collectivist and individualist cultures perceive the world. Table 7.1 summarizes their findings (Masuda & Nisbett, 2001).

> *Individualist and collectivist cultures view the world slightly differently because of how they view themselves.*

TABLE 7.1 WORLDVIEW: INDIVIDUALISTIC VS. COLLECTIVIST CULTURES

INDIVIDUALISTIC CULTURES	COLLECTIVIST CULTURES
• They focus on the self, and their minds focus more on the central object of a picture. • Object change affects eye fixations. • When focusing on images, they are scanning more and not focused on a central object (Rayner et al., 2007). • Objects trigger higher access to prior knowledge. • They are more analytical about objects and emphasize object properties and location.	• They are more likely to recall the background in pictures and have these details hold their attention with equal focus to that of the central object. • Changing the background impacts focus more than changing the main object. • They see themselves as part of a group and tend to focus more broadly. • They are more biased in processing context, utilizing categories less and relying more on intuitive rather than formal reasoning processes.

SOURCE: Masuda & Nisbett (2001).

This study showed how we view ourselves biases how the brain processes the world. This indicates that culture changes brain function on a physiological level. Consider the ramifications. People from different cultures can experience different brain activation processes when viewing the same thing. Cultural differences can influence behavior when people see an object, how motivated a person is to possess an object, and what they might be willing to do to get it.

> *How we view ourselves biases how the brain processes the world.*

CULTURE CAN INFLUENCE HOW WE VIEW ONE ANOTHER

When viewing faces, an interesting juxtaposition occurs between individualist and collectivist cultures. Collectivist cultures focus on a single central region of the face when viewing faces, whereas individualist cultures scan more broadly (Blais et al., 2008). This could reflect gaze avoidance, which is characteristic of many collectivist cultures. Because of this, the ability to discriminate certain facial expressions seems more difficult for people from collectivist cultures (Jack et al., 2009). The conclusion is that culture plays a role in modulating perceptions of emotion. The implication is that cultural differences can negatively influence the communication of emotion across cultures. In addition, both individualist and collectivist cultures demonstrated a greater amygdala activation to the fear expressed by members of their cultural group (Chiao et al., 2008). This might indicate the encoding of cultural preference as an aspect of survival.

> *Culture plays a role in modulating perceptions of emotion.*

CULTURE CAN INFLUENCE HOW WE VIEW THE SELF

Perhaps the most significant distinction between individualist and collectivist cultures is how we view ourselves. When we make judgments about ourselves, the medial prefrontal cortex and anterior cingulate cortex are expected to be activated. However, when people in collectivist cultures make judgments about people like their mothers, the same region associated with self-judgment activates (Zhu et al., 2007). The ability to value the group over the self is not only a cognitive decision and an emotional value; it transforms how the brain views the self.

> *The ability to value the group over the self is not only a cognitive decision and an emotional value; it transforms how the brain views the self.*

The difference between individualist and collectivist cultures was further emphasized when people from collectivist cultures showed lower anterior activity upon seeing pictures of themselves compared to people they know (Sui et al., 2009). The **anterior** is supposed to light up when we see an image of ourselves. In individualist cultures, the activation is high when we see ourselves reflected and lowers dramatically when we see people we know. Participants from collectivist cultures showed a reverse pattern, demonstrating how the view of self and others can be neurally altered by culture. The neural activation occurs between 280 and 340 milliseconds after we see ourselves, indicating that this process has evolved long enough to be almost subconscious. One can conclude that the longer cultural differences are in place, the more significant the impact on brain functions.

> *The longer cultural differences are in place, the more significant the impact on brain functions.*

RECOMMENDATIONS FOR EDUCATORS

1. **Maximize the Benefits of Different Cultural Perspectives in the Workplace**

What it is: People from the dominant culture often share perspectives, and the agreement makes them feel correct in their approach and conclusions. Cultural neuroscience demonstrates that people from different cultures bring a unique perspective and have minds that might do some things better than others. The issue is to look at cultural differences not as a handicap but as an advantage.

What it looks like in practice: The Max Delbrück Center for Molecular Medicine in Berlin, Germany, is a research laboratory that intentionally hires scientists from many world cultures. They decided to maximize the benefits of people viewing things from different perspectives. Here are the steps they recommend:

- Be intentional in recruiting and hiring people from diverse cultures.

- Use tools that anonymize applications. Neuroscience tells us that names, gender, and race trigger automated subconscious responses that influence thoughts and actions.

- Create inclusive job descriptions. Avoid gendered language or terms that might deter certain groups. Clearly state your commitment to diversity and inclusion.

- Foster diversity from the top down. When leadership visibly supports diversity, it sets the tone for the organization.

- Understand that cultures bias our perspectives and influence how we view things. Therefore, we should embrace the differences to produce a better product. The brain often does not consider other approaches once it has determined a preferred method. A simple exercise to consistently do with staff is to brainstorm all the valid ways to achieve an objective. Then, remind them there are always different ways to achieve a desired outcome. This process helps staff recognize that approaches are not usually an issue of best or worst but often a matter of preference. Over time, people become more open to alternative ideas.

- Establish protocols that prevent the dominant culture from determining that the best way to reach a group consensus is always based on a majority vote. Here is a process for considering everyone's ideas.

  o A process or solution is presented to the staff.

  o Staff members place a red dot (thumbs down) or green dot (thumbs up) on the proposal.

  o The recommendation is approved if an item receives all green dots.

  o If the recommendation has any red dots, automatically move to the discussion.

  o Ask each red-dot staff member for their suggestions for improvement. Write all the improvement suggestions on blank chart paper. Bring forth the revised process or solution.

  o If accepted, a modified recommendation is put in place.

  o If not, the original process or solution passes.

2. Maximize the Benefits of Different Cultural Perspectives in the Classroom

What it is: Culturally responsive teaching recognizes the importance of including students' cultural references in the approach to learning. Here are recommended steps for maximizing the benefits of diversity in the classroom.

What it looks like in practice:

- Validate students' prior knowledge: Students enter the classroom with diverse experiences. The ability to express different experiences and knowledge, not as better or worse, validates them. This strategy also allows students to better understand the range of backgrounds their peers come from.

- Connect learning to students' lives: For example, a lesson in history class can be made relevant when students discuss why it matters today or what it would look like if it were to happen now. Whenever connections between the lesson and students' lives can be made, it is not only more culturally competent but will also increase comprehension and recall.

- Capitalize on language and comprehension: In many classrooms today, teachers may have several students who speak different languages. Consider having students teach what the words would be in their native language when learning keywords. Also, have students explain if a word has a different meaning in their culture. This practice increases the sensitivity to learning a new language, as well as that the same word's meaning can vary with culture.

- Make lessons and resources more inclusive: When possible, attempt to have lessons and resources that reflect cultural diversity and neurodiversity. These simple steps make learning more inclusive.

- Build relationships with all students: Culturally responsive teaching is based on building good rapport with students. Developing a good relationship with students ensures that nonverbal communication matches what is said.

Why it works: School climates that embrace the unique perspectives of people from different cultures can benefit education outcomes. Considering things from many perspectives has increased cognitive flexibility and resiliency (Diamond, 2013). Cognitive flexibility is adapting one's thinking and behavior to a changing environment.

CONCLUSION

Our cultures can shape our brains' processes and allow us to see things from different perspectives and approaches. Schools and classrooms that embrace cultural differences can strengthen the workforce and enhance the learning process. The ability to capitalize on the advantages that diversity affords us requires an openness to seeing and trying things differently. Agencies that have made this effort have found that it has improved their worldview and productivity.

CHAPTER 8

....

VICTIM OF SOCIETY

Pervasive Societal Biases

CHAPTER OVERVIEW

▶ Pervasive societal biases are so deeply rooted that most educators subconsciously apply them even to the youngest students, altering these children's first experience with the education system and changing their academic trajectory. However, having an internal desire not to act in a prejudicial manner, coupled with some intentional behaviors, can allow the brain to dampen implicit associations better.

OUR PREATTENTION TO RACE AND BIOLOGICAL SEX

Recall our discussion in Chapter 2 around the preattentional system and how it decides what is most important to focus on in a given environment. This process has become so efficient that it occurs subconsciously. Consequently, this can cause pervasive societal patterns to influence the preattentional system, having significant implications for understanding the activation of race and gender information in the preattentional system.

Researchers found that in the United States, our preattention notices race as early as 100 milliseconds. Gender also emerges early, about 50 milliseconds later than attention to race (Ito & Urland, 2003). The preattention to biological sex is logical. Our need to notice the sex of others is essential for the continuation of the human race. Noticing gender ensures we do not miss individuals we are attracted to; therefore, it is related to survival. What is unique for us in the United States is that, over time, our focus on race became more important to survival than our preattention to biological sex.

> *Over time, our focus on race became more important to survival than our preattention to biological sex.*

How quickly the brain focuses on race and gender is important because we do not encode faces until around 170 milliseconds or retrieve personal identity until around 350 milliseconds (Ito & Urland, 2003). This means that before we experience an empathy response, our preconceived subconscious associations about race and gender will influence subsequent thoughts. Observing a person's face humanizes them by providing an instant, empathetic response to what they are feeling. If another subconscious process that influences our opinions about people precedes the empathy response, then the empathy response is dampened. Highly empathetic people are unaware that their perceptions of certain people differ from how they observe others. That is the sad truth about societal biases; most of us are victims.

When our brains process gender faster than they can produce an empathy response, any unintentional and automatic mental associations based on gender stemming from traditions, norms, values, culture, and experience occur before we see the person. For example, if a young boy is raised in an environment where males consistently sexually objectify women, he then makes the learned automatic associations when viewing females. These automated responses influence actions leading to inappropriate behaviors.

Most professions have particular biases held toward women. For example, the field of higher education has an established bias that women are intellectually inferior to men (Llorens et al., 2021). The outcome is that women hold significantly fewer department chairs than men. A department chair at a university is the person who serves as a leader for their department. However, this bias does not seem evident in K–12 education. The reason might be that women represent 77% of public school teachers (National Center for Education Statistics, 2023).

Nonetheless, the prejudice toward women in leadership positions is still evident across most professions. Two biases are consistently found: Men are inherently better leaders than women, and a woman's mental makeup makes her less emotionally capable of leading than a man (Eagly & Karau, 2002). One consequence is that a female leader is scrutinized more severely and her decisions are questioned to a greater extent. Another consequence is that it is more difficult for women to become leaders because there is a bias to avoid having females in leadership roles. It is likely that viewing men as superior leaders to women is rooted in physical dominance as it relates to survival (Jewkes et al., 2015). In addition, the classic female brain structure tends to utilize the left amygdala more during emotional decision-making (Reber & Tranel, 2017). The left amygdala is prone to emotional consideration. The right, which most men utilize during emotional decision-making, is prone to decisive action (Reber & Tranel, 2017). It is believed that in a male-dominated world, decisive action was viewed as a strength. However, there is a higher connection between the left amygdala and the pre-frontal cortex than on the right during stressful decisions. This leads some researchers to think that women are well suited for leadership positions because the most rational part of the brain might be more active in moments of crisis.

Unfortunately, there is no easy explanation for the occurrence of **implicit racial bias**. It would be a mistake to attribute societal biases related to race as merely a function of in-group preference, which we covered in Chapter 1. Studies show that children as early as age 5 begin to show an **anti-group response** (Hirschfeld, 2008), a negative response to certain out-groups. As early as age 10, children begin to form values and attitudes that conflict with established implicit biases (Baron & Banaji, 2006). This shows that implicit social biases are formulated very early, remain constant throughout life, and are not mitigated by conscious disagreement. Contradictory values and beliefs do not seem to be enough to cause an implicit bias to dissipate.

> *Implicit social biases are formulated very early, remain constant throughout life, and are not mitigated by conscious disagreement.*

The presence of an in-group preference does not automatically produce an adverse reaction to out-group members. Studies have shown that Black Americans display a strong preference to other Black people but, on average, lack an implicit anti-group bias toward white people, specifically (Nosek et al., 2002). And this is consistent across other races as well. In the United States, most people of color do not have an implicit negative response to white people. However, some racial and ethnic minority groups implicitly respond negatively to other minority groups but not to whites. In contrast, up to 80% of white Americans who have taken the

Implicit Association Test show an anti-group response toward other racial and ethnic groups (Baron & Banaji, 2006). This disproportionate reaction indicates that within U.S. society, people of color, particularly Black people, consistently produce a negative implicit response across all racial and ethnic identities.

YOUR BRAIN ON RACE

What is a **social implicit bias**? It is a subconscious decision to perceive a group of people with whom we have no personal history based on associations made in society. The amygdala has been identified as the part of the brain involved in attraction and distrust decisions. As a result, the amygdala's response to people became the focus of many implicit bias studies. These studies tested amygdala response to different groups of people and genders, with the most consistent finding being that, in the United States, there is a heightened amygdala response to Black people indicative of implicit bias. A close examination of these studies indicates how embedded and commonly held implicit biases are associated with Black people.

> *In the United States, there is a heightened amygdala response to Black people indicative of implicit bias.*

One study tested amygdala activation while participants completed a series of trust games with partners of varying races. The study found that there was a significant amygdala activation when participants had to trust a Black participant (Stanley et al., 2012). An implicit lack of trust in Black people has significant social ramifications. If you implicitly distrust Black people, will you want to work side by side with them, teach them, mentor them, cultivate a friendship, or entrust them to do a vital task?

Another study established that most people have a robust amygdala activation when observing out-group members (Hart et al., 2000). However, this study found that amygdala activation intensifies when a subject repeatedly sees in-group members and then sees an out-group member. The conclusion was that the amygdala encodes social and biological data relating to a sense of belonging. This subtle distinction should not be glossed over. There might be a correlation between the intensity of implicit bias and a person's need to belong. In addition, people who live in homogeneous settings will be more likely to have a stronger reaction to the presence of an out-group member. A study found that the more homogeneous the setting, the more implicit racial stereotypes held (Bai et al., 2020).

> *The amygdala encodes social and biological data relating to a sense of belonging.*

> *The more homogeneous the setting, the more implicit racial stereotypes held (Bai et al., 2020).*

Homogeneous settings are linked to a greater sense of belonging; thus, the introduction of an out-group member might threaten the sense of belonging. The **anterior cingulate cortex**, a region of the brain that reacts when someone is experiencing physical and social pain, plays a significant role in social exclusion. Researchers found that the greatest anterior cingulate cortex activation came when a person felt excluded by in-group members (Krill & Platek, 2009). Individuals who demonstrated significant distress to the exclusion showed higher amygdala activation (fear) toward out-group members. This finding might explain the resistance racists and separatists have toward the concept of inclusion. People with the strongest desire for only the advancement of in-group members are driven by the need to belong and the fear of exclusion. Separatism protects the sense of belonging and combats the fear of exclusion. Early work on racism found that racists consistently demonstrated a heightened amygdala response to out-group members, which was indicative of fear (Chekroud et al, 2014). It is likely that extreme reactions to out-group members are indicative of higher levels of activation in both the amygdala and the anterior cingulate cortex.

> *People with the strongest desire for only the advancement of in-group members are driven by the need to belong and the fear of exclusion.*

Implicit and Explicit Racial Bias

Another study that focused on the reaction of the **dorsolateral prefrontal cortex** to implicit and explicit racial bias provided yet another facet to the complexity of social interaction between racial groups. The study found that racial bias predicted the depletion of executive control (Richeson et al., 2003). **Executive control** is the ability of the cortex to maintain control of the more primitive areas of the brain, such as the amygdala. For example, if you lower executive control, you increase emotional response. The higher the level of racial bias, the greater the depletion of executive control. This finding means that white people with *implicit bias* might feel more taxed when interacting with someone who is non-white. As a result, they might subconsciously avoid the experience. However, someone with *explicit bias* will feel overwhelmed by the exposure to someone non-white, leading to emotional outbursts. The depletion of the dorsolateral prefrontal cortex might play a role in a desire for separation. Individuals with an explicit dislike for people of color, particularly Black people, will quickly lose executive control and experience rising levels of emotions. Over time, the topic of race will become an emotionally charged subject because it causes cognitive load.

It should be noted that skin tone also plays a role in the amygdala response. Researchers found that the amygdala activation increases in direct proportion to skin tone (Ronquillo et al., 2007). The darker the skin tone of the face, the greater the level of amygdala activity. Other studies have found a **skin tone bias,** the tendency to prefer light to dark skin. Within the Black community, this could be due to the historical conditioning to prefer lighter skin due to slavery. However, it might have been socially conditioned. During slavery, those with lighter complexions had the perceived privilege of working indoors, while enslaved people with darker skin were required to work outside in the fields. It should be noted that in the Latino community, darker skin tone is associated with a lower degree of privilege and opportunity. According to a Pew Research Center study, 62% of Latinos believe that having a darker skin color hurts their ability to get ahead (Noe-Bustamante et al., 2021). The question then must be asked: Is the bias toward darker-skinned people rooted in skin tone preference?

Consider the existence of a skin tone bias coupled with negative social stereotypes specifically against Black people, and the result is **implicit** and **explicit racial bias.**

Foundational Studies

A study around implicit racial bias showed Black and white faces to participants, coupled with racially stereotypic context. The faces were shown with either violent rap, no music, or death metal music. The clever researchers showed faces at 32 milliseconds and 525 milliseconds, the prior testing implicit response and the later executive control. At 32 milliseconds, Black faces elicited amygdala activation with no music or violent rap, but not with death metal (Forbes et al., 2012).

The reason death metal did not increase implicit response is because it is not commonly associated with Black people. However, at a slower speed, when most people who have an implicit bias can begin to exercise executive control, the amygdala response persisted when coupled with violent rap (Forbes et al., 2012). The researchers concluded that you can prime negative racial stereotype reactions and that it seems to hinder the top-down control of the amygdala. The finding indicates that people who have only an implicit bias are less likely to control implicit reactions in the presence of racial stereotypes. The implications here are immense.

> *People who have only an implicit bias are less likely to control implicit reactions in the presence of racial stereotypes.*

Every time we are exposed to *social stereotypes*, it is hard to suppress *implicit biases*. Seeing a group of Black male students dress in sagging pants, hearing a group of Black boys rapping, and listening to some Black students' use of African American Vernacular English (AAVE) would all diminish a teacher's ability to control implicit biases associated with Black people. When top-down control is diminished, our actions are more likely to reflect our biases. Bias will be noted in the face, hands, posture, and tone of voice. Students would subconsciously notice and then have a negative gut reaction toward the teacher. The teacher would notice the negative reaction, and their biases would intensify. The entire interaction would occur in milliseconds without anyone being the wiser about the social interplay that just transpired.

Exploring explicit racial bias, researchers had white participants view Black and white faces at 30 milliseconds and checked amygdala activation through functional **magnetic resonance imaging** (MRI). The result was greater amygdala activation for Black than white faces (Cunningham et al.,

2004). The amygdala response was significantly reduced when the faces were presented for 525 milliseconds (Cunningham et al., 2004). The reason is that the part of the frontal cortex associated with control and regulation showed greater activation after seeing a Black face. Also, people with more significant racial bias showed greater activation in the amygdala and an inability to regulate this response in the frontal cortex. The result supports the idea that people who are not explicitly biased attempt to regulate implicit reactions. The problem is that negative societal associations dampen the ability to regulate implicit reactions.

THE DANGERS OF ASSOCIATIONS

In the Real World

What associations caused this racial bias? Researchers discovered that implicit racial stereotypes linked danger and threat more strongly to young Black men than to white men (Lundberg et al., 2018). The finding was consistent across Black males of older age. The study found that it was more natural for participants to associate Black people with dangerous objects and words. This is not an isolated finding. Similar results have been found in several other studies (e.g., Eberhardt et al., 2004). The aforementioned experiment was done earlier, using children rather than adolescents and adults. The assumption was made that we as a society view young children differently from adults. Children are viewed as innocent and in need of protection. However, researchers found that white participants still made implicit associations between dangerous objects like a weapon or dangerous words like *violence* and young Black faces (Todd, Simpson, et al., 2016; Todd, Thiem, & Neel, 2016).

> *Implicit racial stereotypes linked danger and threat more strongly to young Black men than to white men (Lundberg et al., 2018).*

The association of negative social stereotypes with young Black children is disturbing. However, when these implicit associations are tested further, they become disheartening. A study confirmed three implicit associations (Goff et al., 2014):

1. Black boys are seen as less "childlike" than their white peers.

2. The characteristics associated with childhood are applied less to Black boys relative to white boys.

3. Black males are dehumanized by associating them (implicitly) with apes. The research suggests that dehumanization behaviors, such as associating Blacks with apes, occur under certain in-group bonding activities.

Recall Chapter 3 where we learned that confirmation bias teaches us that perceptions are reality. The association of Black males with violence is perceived as a threat to the brain. The amygdala's primary function is our survival. The pervasive stereotypes linking Black males with violence and criminality can lead to real-life consequences. Take the experiment conducted in 2016 where participants had to quickly identify if someone was holding a harmless object or a weapon. Researchers concluded that the rate of misidentification of harmless objects as weapons in young Black boys and the high number of missing threatening objects when the subject was white could only be attributed to preexisting pervasive bias linking Black males with violence (Todd, Thiem, & Neel, 2016).

In the Classroom

A similar study was done with middle school teachers. Teachers were shown a picture of a middle school student and asked to review their discipline records and make recommendations. The record indicated that the student had two behavioral incidents. The identical record was given a stereotypical

Black name or a white name. Teachers consistently rated the incidents as more severe and recommended harsher disciplinary action when they were given the record with the picture of a Black student (Okonofua & Eberhardt, 2015). Teachers consistently saw the two incidents differently, depending on race. The researchers concluded that implicit racial stereotypes can lead teachers to escalate their negative responses toward Black students throughout interpersonal encounters.

> *Implicit racial stereotypes can lead teachers to escalate their negative responses toward Black students throughout interpersonal encounters.*

The Yale study found that, even at preschool age, Black boys are subconsciously monitored closely (Gilliam et al., 2016). The increased monitoring denotes an association with threat and the likelihood that young Black males will feel targeted. The inability to see young Black male children as children results in Black preschoolers being 3.6 times as likely as white preschoolers to receive one or more suspensions (U.S. Department of Education, Office for Civil Rights, 2016). Studies have shown that there is an expectation of challenges related to Black students, especially boys (Gilliam et al., 2016). A societal association of Black males with dangerous behaviors and being untrustworthy establishes an adversarial relationship with Black male students. The teacher–student relationship undoubtably can begin with this subconscious assumption that Black students will be challenging until proven otherwise. This alters teachers' responses and desired outcomes—for example, a pattern of harsher reactions and a desire for more punitive consequences for Black students. Ironically, studies have shown that these expectations often come to volition *because* we subconsciously influence the outcome.

> *Even at preschool age, Black boys are subconsciously monitored closely (Gilliam et al., 2016).*

> *Black preschoolers are 3.6 times as likely as white preschoolers to receive one or more suspensions (U.S. Department of Education, Office for Civil Rights, 2016).*

School data have consistently indicated that disproportionate rates of disciplinary referrals and exclusionary practices for Black boys can only be understood through the lens of bias (Skiba et al., 2011). There seems to be some transfer of the bias held toward Black males as associated with violence to Latinos of color after elementary school age. Hispanic students are overrepresented in office referrals and suspensions at the middle and high school levels (Skiba et al., 2011). The high school discipline data for Latino males mirror the data for Black males. However, Latinos are significantly underrepresented at the elementary school level. One theory for the underrepresentation in elementary school is that the history of the association of violence with Latinos is not as long as it is with Blacks. However, the social stereotyping of Latino adolescents and adults as associated with violence has become prevalent. The thought is that, by adolescence, the brain only distinguishes skin tone, no longer making a distinction between Blacks and Latinos of color.

The research of Walter S. Gilliam proves that there is an expectation of challenges related to Black students, especially boys. This expectation increases the conscious and subconscious monitoring of Black students (Gilliam et al., 2016). The expectation of challenging behaviors produces a harsher response when behaviors occur, resulting in a punitive approach to consequences. The societal association of Black males with dangerous behaviors undermines the ability to build a trusting relationship between teacher and student. The relationship begins with subconscious signals of mistrust, increasing the likelihood of confrontation. The problem with such a scenario is that it has been established that expectations often come to volition *because* we subconsciously influence the outcome.

The initial exposure to education can set a long-term precedent. For many Black males, the school experience is often unfavorable, without any empathy from other students, teachers, or administrators as to why they feel unliked and treated differently than other students. Meanwhile, loving, caring teachers are unaware of how pervasively these implicit racial biases held by society are influencing their behavior. The impact of viewing students as criminals is the reason why many education activists bring attention to the "**school-to-prison pipeline**," the national trend wherein Black males leave public schools and enter the juvenile and criminal legal systems. Recent research shows that the association of criminality with Latino males is equal to that with Black males because the rate of leaving public school and entering the legal system is now about the same (Augustin, 2016).

Pervasive implicit associations related to race have ramifications in daily life. Nevertheless, most people are unaware that they hold these associations, are unaware when it influences their behaviors, and would be appalled to learn of its devastating outcomes.

Outside of Project Implicit, there is little neuroscience research on societal bias toward sexual orientation, age, disability, and body weight. The overwhelming work on implicit bias in America is focused on race, in large part due to the country's history of slavery, Jim Crow, and ongoing race conflicts. Implicit biases can change when we learn how the brain produces them and make concerted efforts to adjust our thinking. The news is not all bad; more than 4 million people who completed different forms of the Implicit Association Test over 13 years show that Americans' attitudes toward certain social groups are becoming less biased over time. This finding verifies that implicit attitudes are capable of change. Implicit bias toward gay and lesbian individuals received the highest degree of change, with a 33% decrease in bias (Charlesworth & Banaji, 2019). Bias toward people with a dark skin tone received the lowest drop in implicit bias at 15% (Charlesworth & Banaji, 2019).

RECOMMENDATIONS FOR EDUCATORS

1. **Conduct Gender Bias Perception Surveys**

What it is: One of the most common methods of assessing unconscious gender bias in the workplace is to gather data on people's experiences.

What it looks like in practice: Ask employees to list barriers to women's advancement into leadership roles. The process of considering the issue helps raise awareness and sensitivity.

Why it works: Actively considering an issue from a different perspective enables people to reach new conclusions. Independently reached conclusions increase not only sensitivity but also acceptance.

2. **Conduct Blind Evaluations**

What it is: Eliminating physical attributes can prevent implicit bias from influencing the employee selection process. This is a relatively simple way to minimize bias.

What it looks like in practice:

- Each employment application is assigned a unique code. The cover sheet with identifying information is removed until after the selection process. Selected applicants are then identified by the code on the cover sheet.

- Have clerical staff copy résumés and black out all information that can identify physical attributes.

Why it works: Removing identifiers that can subconsciously bias us promotes a more equitable process.

3. **Be Internally Motivated to Consistently Engage in Actions That Mitigate Pervasive Biases**

What it is: Internal motivation to respond without prejudice means to consistently engage in action to mitigate some of the social stereotypes found in society. Consistent action becomes a habit and is internally motivated by a dopamine response.

What it looks like in practice: This approach requires an awareness of social stereotypes and an intentional plan to act in specific ways.

- View social behavior associated with Black students positively, improving executive control.

- Consistently engage with Black students to cultivate many interpersonal relationships, overcoming subconscious trust issues.

Why it works: Individuals motivated to respond without prejudice for primarily internal reasons are less affected by interracial contact. They demonstrated lower amygdala activation and higher executive control in the presence of Blacks (Richeson et al., 2003).

4. Focus on Having an Empathy Response

What it is: There is evidence that having an empathetic response toward Black individuals counteracts dehumanization, which is one of the root causes of implicit social bias (Dambrun et al., 2014). In addition, increasing empathy toward Blacks will increase executive control about associations made that dehumanize Blacks.

What it looks like in practice:

- Intentionally focus on Black students' faces, hands, posture, gestures, and voice tone in the classroom, in real-world interactions or through TV or film. The focus here is not to monitor but to feel.

- Emphasize empathy toward all people of color and other underrepresented groups in social-emotional learning curriculums.

Why it works: White people tend to notice race before the empathy response occurs, and that results in negative associations dampening the empathy response. Research indicates that the brain will rewire if you practice an empathy response long enough (Jankowiak-Siuda et al., 2011).

5. Learn to Make Positive Associations

What it is: Making a positive association is simply seeing a student and immediately thinking of something positive. The strategy seems only to work for individuals internally motivated to respond without prejudice. Individuals who are not motivated saw no dampening of implicit associations (Richeson et al., 2003).

What it looks like in practice:

- Think of a student who has some math potential. Whenever you see them, think of another student you are very fond of, who also shows excellent math potential.

- Think of a student with poor writing skills but amazing creativity. Whenever you see them, think of a past student who also had poor writing skills but became one of the best English students you ever had.

Why it works: Research has found that making a positive association when viewing Black people dampens implicit biases held in society toward Black people (Allen et al., 2010).

CONCLUSION

Most people's understanding of societal biases focuses on their explicit understandings and feelings. However, patterns influence our brains, and we can develop implicit biases that go against our values. Educators who become aware of how the brain produces implicit bias are best equipped to counteract the outcomes societal biases produce. Although some associations commonly made in society might sadden us, the knowledge should motivate change. The change begins with having high expectations and seeing the best in every student. This change can only be achieved by committing to building meaningful relationships with every student.

CONCLUSION

A Moment of Clarity

What can happen in 200 milliseconds? In a word, everything. Within 200 milliseconds, your subconscious mind has shaped your perceptions and influenced your behaviors. In other words, you have been biased. Our automated biases are rooted in our drive to survive, so it should be no surprise that bias is intricately linked with the amygdala, triggering emotion and action. The amygdala can take control of our face, hands, posture, gestures, and voice tone to convey what we feel subconsciously. The amygdala is also an action system, not a thought system, producing responses that we are either unaware of or do not consciously tie to subconscious thoughts.

Our automated biases are always present, acting as lenses through which we see the world. We are born to weigh negative experiences significantly more than positive ones. We tend to confirm our beliefs because our subconscious dictates how our eyes detect things in our surroundings that support them. We also overestimate the impact of anything we believe to be good or bad. These survival biases can dramatically influence our quality of life if we lose **homeostasis**—chemical balance. When we lose our chemical balance, we view too much of life negatively, become blinded by our beliefs, and constantly predict dire outcomes.

Then, born out of affection and even love, we acquire an in-group preference, which is seen in culture, organizations, and society. Cultures, organizations, and society reflect our in-group preferences, unintentionally favoring some and distrusting others. These biases do not act independently; they become interdependent. They trigger one another, creating a cascading effect that falls from so many directions at such high speeds that we are quickly caught in the undertow without ever knowing that we entered the ocean. This is why bias is a complex issue that can only be understood by learning how our brains produce it.

However, the solutions to counter implicit bias begin with simple actions. Control your face, hands, postures, gestures, and voice tone to convey positive signals whenever you interact with someone who looks different from you. Become intentional in striking a balance to avoid becoming too negative, rigid in your beliefs, and confident in your predictions of the future. Also, find that inner motivation to avoid racially prejudiced actions. The avoidance of racially prejudiced actions is not passive but active and requires making positive associations when you see people of color and improving your executive control by developing meaningful relationships. Accept the science that we all live life on the bias, for it is those who are confident that they do not and will not fall prey to implicit associations who yell with certainty, "I am not biased!"

Imagine the impact if educators were aware of implicit bias and actively addressing it. The adverse outcomes associated with implicit bias could be significantly reduced. Educators can raise their expectations by understanding how implicit bias affects students' academic performance and ensure a fair grading process. This proactive approach can help balance different groups' representation in Advanced Placement and Honors classes. Ultimately, this will improve future outcomes, such as grade point averages, college acceptances, career options, and income levels.

Imagine an education system in which no underrepresented groups were overidentified for special education. Teachers' interactions with all students would be supported by body language and tone of voice that show no preconceived notions. This would lead to consistency in student discipline and eliminate the disproportionate representation of students of color in suspensions and expulsions. Students' self-esteem and teacher–student relationships would be given an excellent opportunity to flourish. This would be the impact of knowing how implicit bias affects education and engaging in proven solutions that positively impact teachers, students, and schools.

REFERENCES

Abelson, R. P., & Kanouse, D. E. (1996). Subjective acceptance of verbal generalizations. In S. Feldman (Ed.), *Cognitive consistency* (pp. 173–199). Academic Press.

Acharya, S., & Shukla, S. (2012). Mirror neurons: Enigma of the metaphysical modular brain. *Journal of Natural Science, Biology and Medicine, 3*(2), 118–118. https://doi.org/10.4103/0976-9668.101878

Achor, S. (2010). *The happiness advantage: How a positive brain fuels success in work and life.* Currency.

Adolphs, R. (2010). What does the amygdala contribute to social cognition? *Annals of the New York Academy of Sciences, 1191*(1), 42–61. https://doi.org/10.1111/j.1749-6632.2010.05445.x

Allen, T. J., Sherman, J. W., & Klauer, K. C. (2010). Social context and the self-regulation of implicit bias. *Group Processes & Intergroup Relations, 13*(2), 137–149. https://doi.org/10.1177/1368430209353635

Allport, G. W. (1954). *The nature of prejudice.* Addison-Wesley.

Arend, R., Gove, F. L., & Sroufe, L. A. (1979). Continuity of individual adaptation from infancy to kindergarten: A predictive study of egoresiliency and curiosity in preschoolers. *Child Development, 50*(4), 950–959. https://doi.org/10.2307/1129319

Augustin, S. (2016, January 14). *Can implicit racial bias flush Black and Latino students down the school-to-prison pipeline?* Lawyers' Committee for Civil Rights Under Law. https://www.lawyerscommittee.org/can-implicit-racial-bias-flush-black-latino-students-school-prison-pipeline/

Awad, S., Debatin, T., & Ziegler, A. (2021). Embodiment: I sat, I felt, I performed: Posture effects on mood and cognitive performance. *Acta Psychologica, 218,* Article 103353. https://doi.org/10.1016/j.actpsy.2021.103353

Bai, X., Ramos, M. R., & Fiske, S. T. (2020). As diversity increases, people paradoxically perceive social groups as more similar. *Proceedings of the National Academy of Sciences of the United States of America, 117*(23), 12741–12749. https://doi.org/10.1073/pnas.2000333117

Bambaeeroo, F., & Shokrpour, N. (2017). The impact of the teachers' non-verbal communication on success in teaching. *Journal of Advances in Medical Education & Professionalism, 5*(2), 51–59.

Banaji, M. R., & Hardin, C. (1994). Affect and memory in retrospective reports. In N. Schwartz & S. Sudman (Eds.), *Autobiographical memory and the validity of retrospective reports* (pp. 71–86). Springer New York.

Bar-Haim, Y., Ziv, T., Lamy, D., & Hodes, R. M. (2006). Nature and nurture in own-race face processing. *Psychological Science, 17*(2), 159–163. https://doi.org/10.1111/j.1467-9280.2006.01679.x

Baron, A. S., & Banaji, M. R. (2006). The development of implicit attitudes. Evidence of race evaluations from ages 6 and 10 and adulthood. *Psychological Science, 17*(1), 53–58. https://doi.org/10.1111/j.1467-9280.2005.01664.x

Barrett, N., McEachin, A., Mills, J. N., & Valant, J. (2017*). Disparities in student discipline by race and family income* (pp. 1–56). Education Research Alliance for New Orleans. educationresearchallianceNOLA.org

Baumeister, R. F., Bratslavsky, E., Finkenauer, C., & Vohs, K. D. (2001). Bad is stronger than good. *Review of General Psychology, 5*(4), 323–370. https://doi.org/10.1037/1089-2680.5.4.323

Baus, C., McAleer, P., Marcoux, K., Belin, P., & Costa, A. (2019). Forming social impressions from voices in native and foreign languages. *Scientific Reports, 9*, Article 414. https://doi.org/10.1038/s41598-018-36518-6

Belsky, J., Spritz, B., & Crnic, K. (1996). Infant attachment security and affective-cognitive information processing at age 3. *Psychological Science, 7*(2), 111–114. https://doi.org/10.1111/j.1467-9280.1996.tb00339.x

Bion, W. R. (1977). *Two papers: The grid and caesura.* Imago Editora. (Reprinted from *Two papers: The grid and caesura*, 1989, Karnac)

Blais, C., Jack, R. E., Scheepers, C., Fiset, D., & Caldara, R. (2008). Culture shapes how we look at faces. *PLoS One, 3*(8), Article e3022. https://doi.org/10.1371/journal.pone.0003022

Breese, A. C., Nickerson, A. B., Lemke, M., Mohr, R., Heidelburg, K., Fredrick, S., & Allen, K. (2023). Examining implicit biases of pre-service educators within a professional development context. *Contemporary School Psychology, 27*(4), 646–661. https://doi.org/10.1007/s40688-023-00456-6

Bronson, G. W. (1968). The development of fear in man and other animals. *Child Development, 39*(2), 409–432.

Brophy, J. E. (1985). Teachers' expectations, motives and goals for working with problem students. In C. Ames and R. Ames (Eds.), *Research on motivation in education: The classroom milieu* (pp. 175–214). Academic Press.

Buehler, R., & McFarland, C. (2001). Intensity bias in affective forecasting: The role of temporal focus. *Personality and Social Psychology Bulletin*, 27(11), 1480–1493. https://doi.org/10.1177/01461672012711009

Cacioppo, J. T., Gardner, W., Berntson, G. (1999). The affect system has parallel and integrative processing components: Form follows function. *Journal of Personality and Social Psychology*, 76(5), 839–855. https://doi.org/10.1037/0022-3514.76.5.839

Cameron, L., Rutland, A., Brown, R., & Douch, R. (2006). Changing children's intergroup attitudes toward refugees: Testing different models of extended contact. *Child Development*, 77(5), 1208–1219. https://doi.org/10.1111/j.1467-8624.2006.00929.x

Carr, L., Iacoboni, M., Dubeau, M. C., Mazziotta, J. C., & Lenzi, G. L. (2003). Neural mechanisms of empathy in humans: a relay from neural systems for imitation to limbic areas. *Proceedings of the National Academy of Sciences of the United States of America*, 100(9), 5497–5502. https://doi.org/10.1073/pnas.0935845100

Carstensen, L. L., & DeLiema, M. (2018). The positivity effect: A negativity bias in youth fades with age. *Current Opinion in Behavioral Sciences*, 19, 7–12. https://doi.org/10.1016/j.cobeha.2017.07.009

Carstensen, L. L., & Mikels, J. A. (2005). At the intersection of emotion and cognition: Aging and the positivity effect. *Current Direction Psychological Science*, 14(3), 117–121. https://doi.org/10.1111/j.0963-7214.2005.00348.x

Carstensen, L. L., Pasupathi, M., Mayr, U., & Nesselroade, J. R. (2000). Emotional experience in everyday life across the adult life span. *Journal of Personality and Social Psychology*, 79(4), 644–655. https://doi.org/10.1037/0022-3514.79.4.644

Carver, L. J., & Vaccaro, B. G. (2007). 12-month-old infants allocate increased neural resources to stimuli associated with negative adult emotion. *Developmental Psychology*, 43(1), 54–69. https://doi.org/10.1037/0012-1649.43.1.54

Cascio, C. N., O'Donnell, M. B., Tinney, F. J., Lieberman, M. D., Taylor, S. E., Strecher, V. J., & Falk, E. B. (2016). Self-affirmation activates brain systems associated with self-related processing and reward and is reinforced by future orientation. *Social Cognitive and Affective Neuroscience*, 11(4), 621–629. https://doi.org/10.1093/scan/nsv136

Charles, S. T., & Pasupathi, M. (2003). Age-related patterns of variability in self-descriptions: implications for everyday affective experience. *Psychology and Aging*, 18(3), 524–536. https://doi.org/10.1037/0882-7974.18.3.524

Charles, S. T., Reynolds, C. A., & Gatz, M. (2001). Age-related differences and change in positive and negative affect over 23 years. *Journal of Personality and Social Psychology*, 80(1), 136–151. https://doi.org/10.1037/0022-3514.80.1.136

Charlesworth, T. E. S., & Banaji, M. R. (2019). Patterns of implicit and explicit attitudes: I. Long-term change and stability from 2007 to 2016. *Psychological Science, 30*(2), 174–192. https://doi.org/10.1177/0956797618813087

Chekroud, A. M., Everett, J. A., Bridge, H., & Hewstone, M. (2014). A review of neuroimaging studies of race-related prejudice: Does amygdala response reflect threat? *Frontiers in Human Neuroscience, 8.* https://doi.org/10.3389/fnhum.2014.00179

Chiao, J. Y., Iidaka, T., Gordon, H. L., Nogawa, J., Bar, M., Aminoff, E., Sadato, N., & Ambady, N. (2008). Cultural specificity in amygdala response to fear faces. *Journal of Cognitive Neuroscience, 20*(12), 2167–2174. https://doi.org/10.1162/jocn.2008.20151

Chu, M., & Hagoort, P. (2014). Synchronization of speech and gesture: Evidence for interaction in action. *Journal of Experimental Psychology: General, 143*(4), 1726–1741. https://doi.org/10.1037/a0036281

Collard, R. R. (1967). Fear of strangers and play behavior in kittens with varied social experience. *Child Development, 38*(3), 877–891. https://doi.org/10.2307/1127265

Collins, N. L. (1996). Working models of attachment: Implications for explanation, emotion, and behavior. *Journal of Personality and Social Psychology, 71*(4), 810–832. https://doi.org/10.1037/0022-3514.71.4.810

Collins, N. L., & Read, S. J. (1990). Adult attachment, working models, and relationship quality in dating couples. *Journal of Personality and Social Psychology, 58*(4), 644–663. https://doi.org/10.1037/0022-3514.58.4.644

Cook, R., Bird, G., Catmur, C., Press, C., & Heyes, C. (2014). Mirror neurons: From origin to function. *The Behavioral and Brain Sciences, 37*(2), 177–192. https://doi.org/10.1017/S0140525X13000903

Courchesne, E., Ganz, L., & Norcia, A. M. (1981). Event-related brain potentials to human faces in infants. *Child Development, 52*(3), 804–811. https://doi.org/10.2307/1129080

Cross, M. P., Acevedo, A. M., Leger, K. A., & Pressman, S. D. (2022). How and why could smiling influence physical health? A conceptual review. *Health Psychology Review, 17*(2), 321–343. https://doi.org/10.1080/17437199.2022.2052740

Cunningham, W. A., Johnson, M. K., Raye, C. L., Gatenby, J. C., Gore, J. C., & Banaji, M. R. (2004). Separable neural components in the processing of Black and white faces. *Psychological Science, 15*(12), 806–813. https://doi.org/10.1111/j.0956-7976.2004.00760.x

Dael, N., Mortillaro, M., & Scherer, K. R. (2012). Emotion expression in body action and posture. *Emotion, 12*, 1085–1101. https://doi.org/10.1037/a0025737

Dambrun, M., Lepage, J. L., & Fayolle, S. (2014). Victims' dehumanization and the alteration of other-oriented empathy within the Immersive

Video Milgram Obedience Experiment. *Psychology, 5*(17), 1941–1953. https://doi.org/10.4236/psych.2014.517197

Dapretto, M., Davies, M. S., Pfeifer, J. H., Scott, A. A., Sigman, M., Bookheimer, S. Y., & Iacoboni, M. (2006). Understanding emotions in others: mirror neuron dysfunction in children with autism spectrum disorders. *Nature Neuroscience, 9*(1), 28–30. https://doi.org/10.1038/nn1611

Davidson, R. J., & Begley, S. (2012). *The emotional life of your brain: How its unique patterns affect the way you think, feel, and live, and how you can change them.* Hudson Street Press.

Davidson, R. J., & Lutz, A. (2008). Buddha's brain: Neuroplasticity and meditation. *IEEE Signal Processing Magazine, 25*(1), 176–174. https://doi.org/10.1109/msp.2008.4431873

Diamond, A. (2013). Executive functions. *Annual Review of Psychology, 64,* 135–168. https://doi.org/10.1146/annurev-psych-113011-143750

Dichter, B. K., Breshears, J. D., Leonard, M. K., & Chang, E. F. (2018). The control of vocal pitch in human laryngeal motor cortex. *Cell, 174*(1), 21–31.e9. https://doi.org/10.1016/j.cell.2018.05.016

Dimberg, U., Thunberg, M., & Elmehed, K. (2000). Unconscious facial reactions to emotional facial expressions. *Psychological Science, 11*(1), 86–89. https://doi.org/10.1111/1467-9280.00221

Dougal, S., & Rotello, C. M. (2007). "Remembering" emotional words is based on response bias, not recollection. *Psychonomic Bulletin and Review, 14,* 423–429. https://doi.org/10.3758/BF03194083

Dreben, E. K., Fiske, S. T., & Hastie, R. (1979). The independence of evaluative and item information: Impression and recall order effects in behavior-based impression formation. *Journal of Personality and Social Psychology, 37*(10), 1758–1768. https://doi.org/10.1037/0022-3514.37.10.1758

Ducette, J., & Soucar, E. (1974). A further reexamination of the vigilance hypothesis with the use of random shapes as stimuli. *The Journal of social psychology, 92*(1), 109–113. https://doi.org/10.1080/00224545.1974.9923078

Eagly, A. H., & Karau, S. J. (2002). Role congruity theory of prejudice toward female leaders. *Psychological Review, 109*(3), 573–598. https://doi.org/10.1037/0033-295x.109.3.573

Eberhardt, J. L., Goff, P. A., Purdie, V. J., & Davies, P. G. (2004). Seeing black: Race, crime, and visual processing. *Journal of Personality and Social Psychology, 87*(6), 876–893. https://doi.org/10.1037/0022-3514.87.6.876

Ekman, P. (2003). *Emotions revealed: Recognizing faces and feelings to improve communication and emotional life.* Henry Holt & Co.

Eysenck, M. W., & Keane, M. T. (2015). *Cognitive psychology: A student's handbook.* Psychology Press.

Fay, N., Walker, B., Ellison, T. M., Blundell, Z., De Kleine, N., Garde, M., Lister, C. J., & Goldin-Meadow, S. (2022). Gesture is the primary modality for language creation. Proceedings. *Biological Sciences*, *289*(1970), Article 20220066. https://doi.org/10.1098/rspb.2022.0066

Fecteau, S., Belin, P., Joanette, Y., & Armony, J. L. (2007). Amygdala responses to nonlinguistic emotional vocalizations. *Neuroimage*, *36*(2), 480–487. https://doi.org/10.1016/j.neuroimage.2007.02.043.

Feeney, B. C, & Kirkpatrick, L. A. (1996). Effects of adult attachment and presence of romantic partners on physiological responses to stress. *Journal of Personality and Social Psychology*, *70*(2), 255–270. https://doi.org/10.1037/0022-3514.70.2.255

Feldman, R., Magori-Cohen, R., Galili, G., Singer, M., Louzoun, Y. (2011). Mother and infant coordinate heart rhythms through episodes of interaction synchrony. *Infant Behavior and Development*, *34*(4), 569–577. https://doi.org/10.1016/j.infbeh.2011.06.008

Ferguson, A. A. (2001). *Bad boys: Public schools in the making of Black masculinity*. University of Michigan Press.

Fiske, S. T. (1980). Attention and weight in person perception: The impact of negative and extreme behavior. *Journal of Personality and Social Psychology*, *38*(6), 889–906. https://doi.org/10.1037/0022-3514.38.6.889

Fiske, S. T., & Taylor, S. E. (1991). *Social cognition* (2nd ed.). McGraw-Hill.

Flaisch, T., Häcker, F., Renner, B., & Schupp, H. T. (2011). Emotion and the processing of symbolic gestures: An event-related brain potential study. *Social Cognitive and Affective Neuroscience*, *6*(1), 109–118. https://doi.org/10.1093/scan/nsq022

Flaisch, T., Schupp, H. T., Renner, B., & Junghöfer, M. (2009). Neural systems of visual attention responding to emotional gestures. *NeuroImage*, *45*(4), 1339–1346. https://doi.org/10.1016/j.neuroimage.2008.12.073

Forbes, C. E., Cox, C. L., Schmader, T., & Ryan, L. (2012). Negative stereotype activation alters interaction between neural correlates of arousal, inhibition and cognitive control. *Social Cognitive and Affective Neuroscience*, *7*(7), 771–781. https://doi.org/10.1093/scan/nsr052

Fugate, M., Prussia, G. E., & Kinicki, A. J. (2012). Managing employee withdrawal during organizational change: The role of threat appraisal. *Journal of Management*, *38*(3), 890–914. https://doi.org/10.1177/0149206309352881

Gaylord-Harden, N. K., Barbarin, O., Tolan, P. H., & Murry, V. M. (2018). Understanding development of African American boys and young men: Moving from risks to positive youth development. *American Psychologist*, *73*(6), 753–767. https://doi.org/10.1037/amp0000300

Gilliam, W. S., Maupin, A. N., Reyes, C. R., Accavitti, M., & Shic, F. (2016). *Do early educators' implicit biases regarding sex and race relate to behavior expectations and recommendations of preschool expulsions and suspensions?* Yale University, Child Study Center.

Goff, P. A., Jackson, M. C., Di Leone, B. A., Culotta, C. M., & DiTomasso, N. A. (2014). The essence of innocence: Consequences of dehumanizing Black children. *Journal of Personality and Social Psychology*, *106*(4), 526–545. https://doi.org/10.1037/a0035663

Grella, S. L., Fortin, A. H., Ruesch, E., Bladon, J. H., Reynolds, L. F., Gross, A., Shpokayte, M., Cincotta, C., Zaki, Y., & Ramirez, S. (2022). Reactivating hippocampal-mediated memories during reconsolidation to disrupt fear. *Nature Communications*, *13*(1), 4733. https://doi .org/10.1038/s41467-022-32246-8

Gross, A. L., & Ballif, B. L. (1991). Children's understanding of emotion from facial expressions and situations: A review. *Developmental Review*, *11*(4), 368–398.

Gross, S. (2010). Origins of human communication - by Michael Tomasello. *Mind & Language*, *25*(2), 237–246. https://doi.org/10.1111/j.1468-0017.2009.01388.x

Gunnar, M. R., Morison, S. J., Chisholm, K. I. M., & Schuder, M. (2001). Salivary cortisol levels in children adopted from Romanian orphanages. *Development and Psychopathology*, *13*(3), 611–628. https://doi .org/10.1017/s095457940100311x

Hamre, B. K., & Pianta, R. C. (2001). Early teacher-child relationships and the trajectory of children's school outcomes through eighth grade. *Child Development*, *72*(2), 625–638. https://doi.org/ 10.1111/1467-8624.00301

Hart, A. J., Whalen, P. J., Shin, L. M., McInerney, S. C., Fischer, H., & Rauch, S. L. (2000). Differential response in the human amygdala to racial outgroup vs ingroup face stimuli. *Neuroreport*, *11*(11), 2351–2355. https://doi.org/10.1097/00001756-200008030-00004

Heron-Delaney, M., Anzures, G., Herbert, J. S., Quinn, P. C., Slater, A., Tanaka, J., Lee, K., & Pascalis, O. (2011). Perceptual training prevents the emergence of the other race effect during infancy. *PLoS One*, *6*(5), Articlee19858. https://doi.org/10.1371/journal.pone.0019858

Herrnstein, R. J., & Murray, C. A. (1994). *The bell curve: Intelligence and class structure in American life*. Free Press.

Hertenstein, M. J., & Campos, J. J. (2004). The retention effects of an adult's emotional displays on infant behavior. *Child Development*, *75*(2), 595–613. https://doi.org/10.1111/j.1467-8624.2004.00695.x

Hiatt, B. (2011, August 4). The neurotic zen of Larry David. *Rolling Stone*. https://www.rollingstone.com/music/music-news/the-neurotic-zen-of-larry-david-165644/

Hirschfeld, L. A. (2008). Children's developing conceptions of race. In S. M. Quintana & C. McKown (Eds.), *Handbook of race, racism, and the developing child* (pp. 37–54). John Wiley & Sons, Inc.

Hornik, R., Risenhoover, N., & Gunnar, M. (1987). The effects of maternal positive, neutral, and negative affective communications on infant responses to new toys. *Child Development, 58*(4), 937–944. https://doi.org/10.2307/1130534

Hu, B. Y., Guo, Y., Wang, S., & Vitiello, V. E. (2021). The associations between teacher-child relationships and academic skills: A longitudinal study among Chinese preschool children. *Contemporary Educational Psychology, 67*(2), Article 102020. https://doi.org/10.1016/j.cedpsych.2021.102020

Huston, T. L., Caughlin, J. P., Houts, R. M., Smith, S. E., & George, L. J. (2001). The connubial crucible: newlywed years as predictors of marital delight, distress, and divorce. *Journal of Personality and Social Psychology, 80*(2), 237–252. https://doi.org/10.1037/0022-3514.80.2.237

İnan-Kaya, G., & Rubie-Davies, C. M. (2022). Teacher classroom interactions and behaviours: Indications of bias. *Learning and Instruction, 78,* Article 101516. https://doi.org/10.1016/j.learninstruc.2021.101516

Ito, T. A., Larsen, J. T., Smith, N. K., & Cacioppo, J. T. (1998). Negative information weighs more heavily on the brain: The negativity bias in evaluative categorizations. *Journal of Personality and Social Psychology, 75*(4), 887–900. https://doi.org/10.1037/0022-3514.75.4.887

Ito, T. A., & Urland, G. R. (2003). Race and gender on the brain: electrocortical measures of attention to the race and gender of multiply categorizable individuals. *Journal of Personality and Social Psychology, 85*(4), 616–626. https://doi.org/10.1037/0022-3514.85.4.616

Jack, R. E., Blais, C., Scheepers, C., Schyns, P. G., & Caldara, R. (2009). Cultural confusions show that facial expressions are not universal. *Current Biology, 19*(18), 1543–1548. https://doi.org/10.1016/j.cub.2009.07.051

Jankowiak-Siuda, K., Rymarczyk, K., & Grabowska, A. (2011). How we empathize with others: A neurobiological perspective. *Medical Science Monitor: International Medical Journal of Experimental and Clinical Research, 17*(1), RA18–RA24. https://doi.org/10.12659/msm.881324

Jeon, H., & Lee, S. H. (2018). From neurons to social beings: Short review of the mirror neuron system research and its sociopsychological and psychiatric implications. *Clinical Psychopharmacology and Neuroscience: The Official Scientific Journal of the Korean College of Neuropsychopharmacology, 16*(1), 18–31. https://doi.org/10.9758/cpn.2018.16.1.18

Jewkes, R., Morrell, R., Hearn, J., Lundqvist, E., Blackbeard, D., Lindegger, G., Quayle, M., Sikweyiya, Y., & Gottzén, L. (2015). Hegemonic masculinity: Combining theory and practice in gender interventions. *Culture, Health & Sexuality, 17*(Suppl. 2), S112–S127. https://doi.org/10.1080/13691058.2015.1085094

Jonsson, F. U., Olsson, H., & Olsson, M. J. (2005). Odor emotionality affects the confidence in odor naming. *Chemical Senses, 30*(1), 29–35. https://doi.org/10.1093/chemse/bjh254

Jou, R. J., Minshew, N. J., Keshavan, M. S., Vitale, M. P., & Hardan, A. Y. (2010). Enlarged right superior temporal gyrus in children and adolescents with autism. *Brain Research*, *1360*, 205–212. https://doi.org/10.1016/j.brainres.2010.09.005

Kahneman, D., & Tversky, A. (1984). Choices, values, and frames. *American Psychologist*, *39*(4), 341–350. https://doi.org/10.1037/0003-066X.39.4.341

Kanouse, D. E., & Hanson, L. R. (1972). Negativity in evaluations. In E. E. Jones, D. E. Kanouse, H. H. Kelley, R. E. Nisbett, S. Valins, & B. Weiner (Eds.), *Attribution: Perceiving the causes of behavior* (pp. 47–62). General Learning.

Kensinger, E. A. (2009). Remembering the details: Effects of emotion. *Emotion Review*, *1*(2), 99. https://doi.org/10.1177/1754073908100432

Kensinger, E. A., & Schacter, D. L. (2008). Memory and emotion. In M. Lewis, J. M. Haviland-Jones, & L. F. Barrett (Eds.), *Handbook of emotions* (3rd ed., pp. 601–617). Guilford Press.

Kiken, L. G., & Shook, N. J. (2011). Looking up: Mindfulness increases positive judgments and reduces negativity bias. *Social Psychological and Personality Science*, *2*(4), 425–431. https://doi.org/10.1177/1948550610396585

Kolb, B., Wilson, B., & Taylor, L. (1992). Developmental changes in the recognition and comprehension of facial expression: Implications for frontal lobe function. *Brain and Cognition*, *20*(1), 74–84. https://doi.org/10.1016/0278-2626(92)90062-q

Koriat, A., Lichtenstein, S., & Fischhoff, B. (1980). Reasons for confidence. *Journal of Experimental Psychology: Human Learning and Memory*, *6*(2), 107–118. https://doi.org/10.1037/0278-7393.6.2.107

Kraft-Todd, G. T., Reinero, D. A., Kelley, J. M., Heberlein, A. S., Baer, L., & Riess, H. (2017). Empathic nonverbal behavior increases ratings of both warmth and competence in a medical context. *PLoS One*, *12*(5), Article e0177758. https://doi.org/10.1371/journal.pone.0177758

Krill, A., & Platek, S. M. (2009). In-group and out-group membership mediates anterior cingulate activation to social exclusion. *Frontiers in Evolutionary Neuroscience*, *1*, 1. https://doi.org/10.3389/neuro.18.001.2009

Kuehne, M., Zaehle, T., & Lobmaier, J. S. (2021). Effects of posed smiling on memory for happy and sad facial expressions. *Scientific Reports*, *11*. https://doi.org/10.1038/s41598-021-89828-7

Lagattuta, K. H., & Wellman, H. M. (2002). Differences in early parent-child conversations about negative versus positive emotions: Implications for the development of psychological understanding. *Developmental Psychology*, *38*(4), 564–580. https://doi.org/10.1037/0012-1649.38.4.564

Langlois, J. H., Ritter, J. M., Roggman, L. A., & Vaughn, L. S. (1991). Facial diversity and infant preferences for attractive faces. *Developmental Psychology*, *27*(1), 79–84. https://doi.org/10.1037/0012-1649.27.1.79

Larsen, J. T., McGraw, P., & Cacioppo, J. T. (2001). Can people feel happy and sad at the same time? *Journal of Personality and Social Psychology*, *81*(4), 684–698.

Lee, K., Quinn, P. C., & Pascalis, O. (2017). Face race processing and racial bias in early development: A perceptual-social linkage. *Current Directions in Psychological Science*, *26*(3), 256–262. https://doi .org/10.1177/0963721417690276

Lee, T. I., Jenner, R. G., Boyer, L. A., Guenther, M. G., Levine, S. S., Kumar, R. M., Chevalier, B., Johnstone, S. E., Cole, M. F., Isono, K.-I., Koseki, H., Fuchikami, T., Abe, K., Murray, H. L., Zucker, J. P., Yuan, B., Bell, G. W., Herbolsheimer, E., Hannett, N. M., . . . & Young, R. A. (2006). Control of developmental regulators by Polycomb in human embryonic stem cells. *Cell*, *125*(2), 301–313. https://doi.org/10.1016/j .cell.2006.02.043

Lee, T. W., Dolan R. J., & Critchley H. D. (2008). Controlling emotional expression: behavioral and neural correlates of nonimitative emotional responses. *Cerebral Cortex*, *18*(1), 104–113. https://doi.org/10.1093/ cercor/bhm035

Leong, D. (2024). Organizational homeostasis: A quantum theoretical exploration with bohmian and prigoginian systemic insights. *Qeios*. https:// doi.org/10.32388/4R1VW5.2Levenson, R. W., & Gottman, J. M. (1985). Physiological and affective predictors of change in relationship satisfaction. *Journal of Personality and Social Psychology*, *49*(1), 85–94. https://doi.org/10.1037//0022-3514.49.1.85

Lieberman, P. (2007). The evolution of human speech. *Current Anthropology*, *48*(1), 39–66. https://doi.org/10.1086/509092

Llorens, A., Tzovara, A., Bellier, L., Bhaya-Grossman, I., Bidet-Caulet, A., Chang, W. K., Cross, Z. R., Dominguez-Faus, R., Flinker, A., Fonken, Y., Gorenstein, M. A., Holdgraf, C., Hoy, C. W., Ivanova, M. V., Jimenez, R. T., Jun, S., Kam, J. W. Y., Kidd, C., Marcelle, E., Marciano, D., . . . Dronkers, N. F. (2021). Gender bias in academia: A lifetime problem that needs solutions. *Neuron*, *109*(13), 2047–2074. https://doi. org/10.1016/j.neuron.2021.06.002

Loftus, E. F. (2005). Planting misinformation in the human mind: a 30-year investigation of the malleability of memory. *Learning & Memory*, *12*(4), 361–366. https://doi.org/10.1101/lm.94705

Lopez, L. D., Reschke, P. J., Knothe, J. M., & Walle, E. A. (2017). Postural communication of emotion: Perception of distinct poses of five discrete emotions. *Frontiers in Psychology*, *8*. https://doi.org/10.3389/ fpsyg.2017.00710

Lundberg, G. J. W., Neel, R., Lassetter, B., & Todd, A. R. (2018). Racial bias in implicit danger associations generalizes to older male targets.

PloS One, 13(6), Article e0197398. https://doi.org/10.1371/journal .pone.0197398

Lutz, A., Dunne, J. P., & Davidson, R. J. (2006). Meditation and the neuroscience of consciousness: An introduction. In P. D. Zelazo & E. Thompson (Eds.), *The Cambridge handbook of consciousness* (pp. 497–549). Cambridge University Press.

Lutz, A., Greischar, L., Rawlings, N. B., Ricard, M., & Davidson, R. J. (2004). Long-term meditators self-induce high-amplitude synchrony during mental practice. *Proceedings of the National Academy of Sciences, 101*(46), 16369–16373. https://doi.org/10.1073/pnas.0407401101

Malatesta, C. (1985). The developmental course of emotion expression in the human infant. In G. Zivin (Ed.), *Expressive development: Biological and environmental interactions* (pp. 183–220). Academic Press.

Manning, J. T., Scutt, D., Wilson, J., & Lewis-Jones, D. I. (1998). The ratio of 2nd to 4th digit length: A predictor of sperm numbers and concentrations of testosterone, luteinizing hormone and oestrogen. *Human Reproduction, 13*(11), 3000–3004. 10.1093/humrep/13.11.3000

Marques, A. J., Gomes Veloso, P., Araújo, M., de Almeida, R. S., Correia, A., Pereira, J., Queiros, C., Pimenta, R., Pereira, A. S., & Silva, C. F. (2022). Impact of a virtual reality-based simulation on empathy and attitudes toward schizophrenia. *Frontiers in Psychology, 13*, Article 814984. https://doi.org/10.3389/fpsyg.2022.814984

Marstaller, L., & Burianová, H. (2013). Individual differences in the gesture effect on working memory. *Psychonomic Bulletin & Review, 20*(3), 496–500. https://doi.org/10.3758/s13423-012-0365-0

Martinez-Conde, S., & Macknik, S. L. (2007). Windows on the mind. *Scientific American, 297*(2), 56–63. https://doi.org/10.1038/scientific american0807-56

Mather, M., & Carstensen, L. L. (2005). Aging and motivated cognition: The positivity effect in attention and memory. *Trends in Cognitive Sciences, 9*(10), 496–502. https://doi.org/10.1016/j.tics.2005.08.005

Masuda, T., & Nisbett, R. E. (2001). Attending holistically versus analytically: Comparing the context sensitivity of Japanese and Americans. *Journal of Personality and Social Psychology, 81*(5), 922–934. https:// doi.org/10.1037/0022-3514.81.5.922

Matsumoto, D., & Hwang, H. S. (2011). Judgments of facial expressions of emotion in profile. *Emotion, 11*(5), 1223–1229. https://doi .org/10.1037/a0024356

McEwen, B. S. (2017). Neurobiological and systemic effects of chronic stress. *Chronic Stress.* Advance online publication. https://doi.org/10.1177/ 2470547017692328

McGaugh, J. L. (2000). Memory—a century of consolidation. *Science, 287*(5451), 248–251. https://doi.org/10.1126/science.287 .5451.248

McIntyre, M. H. (2006). The use of digit ratios as markers for perinatal androgen action. *Reproductive Biology and Endocrinology, 4*(1), 10.

Meaney, M. J., & Szyf, M. (2005). Maternal care as a model for experience-dependent chromatin plasticity? *Trends in Neurosciences, 28*(9), 456–463. https://doi.org/10.1016/j.tins.2005.07.006

Mercier, H. (2016). The argumentative theory: Predictions and empirical evidence. *Trends in Cognitive Sciences, 20*(9), 689–700. https://doi.org/10.1016/j.tics.2016.07.001

Meyer, F., Bendikson, L., & Le Fevre, D. M. (2023). Leading school improvement through goal-setting: Evidence from New Zealand schools. *Educational Management Administration & Leadership, 51*(2), 365–383. https://doi.org/10.1177/1741143220979711

Mikulincer, M., & Florian, V. (1998). The relationship between adult attachment styles and emotional and cognitive reactions to stressful events. In J. A. Simpson & W. S. Rholes (Eds.), *Attachment theory and close relationships* (pp. 143–165). Guilford Press.

Morewedge, C. K., & Buechel, E. C. (2013). Motivated underpinnings of the impact bias in affective forecasts. *Emotion, 13*(6), 1023–1029. https://doi.org/10.1037/a0033797

Moss, E., Gosselin, C, Parent, S., Rousseau, D., & Dumont, M. (1997). Attachment and joint problem-solving experiences during the preschool period. *Social Development, 6*(1), 1–17. https://doi.org/10.1111/j.1467-9507.1997.tb00091.x

Muehlhan, M., Marxen, M., Landsiedel, J., Malberg, H., & Zaunseder, S. (2014). The effect of body posture on cognitive performance: A question of sleep quality. *Frontiers in Human Neuroscience, 8*, 171. https://doi.org/10.3389/fnhum.2014.00171

Mumme, D. L., Fernald, A., & Herrera, C. (1996). Infants' responses to facial and vocal emotional signals in a social referencing paradigm. *Child Development, 67*(6), 3219–3237.

Myers, D. G. (1982). Polarizing effects of social interaction, in group decision making. In H. Brandstätter, J. H. Davis, & G. Stocker-Kreichgauer (Eds.), *Group decision making* (pp. 125–161). Academic Press.

Načinović Braje, I., Klindžić, M. & Galetić, L. (2019). The role of individual variable pay in a collectivistic culture society: An evaluation. *Economic Research–Ekonomska Istraživanja, 32*(1), 1352–1372. https://doi.org/10.1080/1331677X.2018.1559073

National Center for Education Statistics. (2023). Characteristics of public school teachers. *Condition of Education.* U.S. Department of Education, Institute of Education Sciences. https://nces.ed.gov/programs/coe/indicator/clr

Nelson, C. A. (1994). Neurocorrelates of recognition memory in the first postnatal year of life. In G. Dawson & K. Fischer (Eds.), *Human behavior and the developing brain* (pp. 269–313). Guilford Press.

Nickerson, R. S. (1998). Confirmation bias: A ubiquitous phenomenon in many guises. *Review of General Psychology, 2*(2), 175–220. https://doi.org/10.1037/1089-2680.2.2.175

Noe-Bustamante, L., Gonzalez-Barrera, A., Edwards, K., Mora, L., & Lopez, M. H. (2021, November 4). *Majority of Latinos say skin color impacts opportunity in America and shapes daily life.* Pew Research Center. https://www.pewresearch.org/race-and-ethnicity/2021/11/04/majority-of-latinos-say-skin-color-impacts-opportunity-in-america-and-shapes-daily-life/

Norris, C. J., Leaf, P. T., & Fenn, K. M. (2019). Negativity bias in false memory: Moderation by neuroticism after a delay. *Cognition & Emotion, 33*(4), 737–753. https://doi.org/10.1080/02699931.2018.1496068

Nosek, B. A., Banaji, M. R., & Greenwald, A. G. (2002). Harvesting implicit group attitudes and beliefs from a demonstration web site. *Group Dynamics: Theory, Research, and Practice, 6*(1), 101–115. https://doi.org/10.1037/1089-2699.6.1.101

Oberman, L. M., & Ramachandran, V. S. (2007). The simulating social mind: The role of the mirror neuron system and simulation in the social and communicative deficits of autism spectrum disorders. *Psychological Bulletin, 133*(2), 310–327. https://doi.org/10.1037/0033-2909.133.2.310

Okonofua, J. A., & Eberhardt, J. L. (2015). Two strikes: Race and the disciplining of young students. *Psychological Science, 26*(5), 617–624. https://doi.org/10.1177/0956797615570365

Okura, K. (2022). Stereotype promise: Racialized teacher appraisals of Asian American academic achievement. *Sociology of Education, 95*(4), 302–319. https://doi.org/10.1177/00380407221119746

Oyserman, D., Coon, H. M., & Kemmelmeier, M. (2002). Rethinking individualism and collectivism: Evaluation of theoretical assumptions and meta-analyses. *Psychological Bulletin, 128*(1), 3–72. https://doi.org/10.1037/0033-2909.128.1.3

Peeters, G. (1971). The positive-negative asymmetry: On cognitive consistency and positivity bias. *European Journal of Social Psychology, 1*(4), 455–474. https://doi.org/10.1002/ejsp.2420010405

Peeters, G., & Czapinski, J. (1990). Positive–negative asymmetry in evaluations: The distinction between affective and informational negativity effects. In W. Stroebe & M. Hewstone (Eds.), *European review of social psychology* (Vol. 1, pp. 33–60). Wiley.

Penagos-Corzo, J. C., Cosio van-Hasselt, M., Escobar, D., Vázquez-Roque, R. A., & Flores, G. (2022). Mirror neurons and empathy-related regions in psychopathy: Systematic review, meta-analysis, and a working model. *Social Neuroscience, 17*(5), 462–479. https://doi.org/10.1080/17470919.2022.2128868

Peng, W., Lou, W., Huang, X., Ye, Q., Tong, R. K., & Cui, F. (2021). Suffer together, bond together: Brain-to-brain synchronization and mutual affective empathy when sharing painful experiences. *NeuroImage, 238,* Article 118249. https://doi.org/10.1016/j.neuroimage.2021.118249

Pennebaker, J. W. (2017). Expressive writing in psychological science. *Perspectives on Psychological Science, 13*(2). https://doi.org/10.1177/1745691617707315

Phillips, L. H., Henry, J. D., Hosie, J. A., & Milne, A. B. (2008). Effective regulation of the experience and expression of negative affect in old age. *The Journals of Gerontology, Series B: Psychological Sciences and Social Sciences, 63*(3), P138–P145. https://doi.org/10.1093/geronb/63.3.p138

Pinker, S. (1994). *The language instinct.* William Morrow.

Pratto, F., & John, O. P. (1991). Automatic vigilance: The attention-grabbing power of negative social information. *Journal of Personality and Social Psychology, 61*(3), 380–391. https://doi.org/10.1037/0022-3514.61.3.380

Prochazkova, E., & Kret, M. E. (2017). Connecting minds and sharing emotions through mimicry: A neurocognitive model of emotional contagion. *Neuroscience & Biobehavioral Reviews, 80,* 99–114. https://doi.org/10.1016/j.neubiorev.2017.05.013

Quereshi, A., & Okonofua, J. (2017, Winter). Locked out of the classroom: How implicit bias contributes to disparities in school discipline. *Thurgood Marshall Institute: Education Equity No. 2.* https://doi.org/10.2139/ssrn.4702736

Ramos-Cabo, S., Vulchanov, V., & Vulchanova, M. (2019). Gesture and language trajectories in early development: An overview from the autism spectrum disorder perspective. *Frontiers in Psychology, 10,* 1211. https://doi.org/10.3389/fpsyg.2019.01211

Rank, O. (1929). *The trauma of birth.* Courier Corporation.

Rasmussen, B., & Bliss, S. (2014). Beneath the surface: An exploration of neurobiological alterations in therapists working with trauma. *Smith College Studies in Social Work, 84*(2–3), 332–349. https://doi.org/10.1080/00377317.2014.923714

Rayner, K., Li, X., Williams, C. C., Cave, K. R., & Well, A. D. (2007). Eye movements during information processing tasks: Individual differences and cultural effects. *Vision Research, 47*(21), 2714–2726. https://doi.org/10.1016/j.visres.2007.05.007

Reber, J., & Tranel, D. (2017). Sex differences in the functional lateralization of emotion and decision making in the human brain. *Journal of Neuroscience Research, 95*(1–2), 270–278. https://doi.org/10.1002/jnr.23829

Regev, G., Hayard, O., & Wegmann, A. (2013). What we can learn about business modeling from homeostasis. In B. Shishkov (Eds.), *Business modeling and software design.* BMSD 2012. Lecture Notes in Business

Information Processing, vol. 142. Springer, Berlin, Heidelberg. https://doi.org/10.1007/978-3-642-37478-4_1

Richeson, J. A., Baird, A. A., Gordon, H. L., Heatherton, T. F., Wyland, C. L., Trawalter, S., & Shelton, J. N. (2003). An fMRI investigation of the impact of interracial contact on executive function. *Nature Neuroscience, 6*(12), 1323–1328. https://doi.org/10.1038/nn1156

Riess, H. (2017). The science of empathy. *Journal of Patient Experience, 4*(2), 74–77. https://doi.org/10.1177/2374373517699267

Rizzolatti, G., & Craighero, L. (2004). The mirror-neuron system. *Annual Review of Neuroscience, 27*, 169–192. https://doi.org/10.1146/annurev.neuro.27.070203.144230

Robinson, M. D., & Clore, G. L. (2001). Simulation, scenarios, and emotional appraisal: Testing the convergence of real and imagined reactions to emotional stimuli. *Personality & Social Psychology Bulletin, 27*(11), 1520–1532. https://doi.org/10.1177/01461672012711012

Ronquillo, J., Denson, T. F., Lickel, B., Lu, Z. L., Nandy, A., & Maddox, K. B. (2007). The effects of skin tone on race-related amygdala activity: an fMRI investigation. *Social Cognitive and Affective Neuroscience, 2*(1), 39–44. https://doi.org/10.1093/scan/nsl043

Rosenthal, R., & Jacobson, L. (1966). Teachers' expectancies: Determinants of pupils' IQ gains. *Psychological Reports, 19*(1), 115–118. https://doi.org/10.2466/pr0.1966.19.1.115

Rosenthal, R., & Jacobson, L. (1992). *Pygmalion in the classroom* (Expanded ed.). Irvington.

Roswandowitz, C., Kappes, C., Obrig, H., & von Kriegstein, K. (2018). Obligatory and facultative brain regions for voice-identity recognition. *Brain: A Journal of Neurology, 141*(1), 234–247. https://doi.org/10.1093/brain/awx313

Rozin, P., & Royzman, E. B. (2001). Negativity bias, negativity dominance, and contagion. *Personality and Social Psychology Review, 5*(4), 296–320. https://doi.org/10.1207/S15327957PSPR0504_2

Rupp, K., Hect, J. L., Remick, M., Ghuman, A., Chandrasekaran, B., Holt, L. L., & Abel, T. J. (2022). Neural responses in human superior temporal cortex support coding of voice representations. *PLoS Biology, 20*(7), Article e3001675. https://doi.org/10.1371/journal.pbio.3001675

Sangrigoli, S., & De Schonen, S. (2004). Recognition of own-race and other-race faces by three-month-old infants. *Journal of Child Psychology and Psychiatry, and Allied Disciplines, 45*(7), 1219–1227. https://doi.org/10.1111/j.1469-7610.2004.00319.x

Sapienza, P., Zingales, L., & Maestripieri, D. (2009). Gender differences in financial risk aversion and career choices are affected by testosterone. *Proceedings of the National Academy of Sciences of the United States of America, 106*(36), 15268–15273. https://doi.org/10.1073/pnas.0907352106

Schmack, K., Rössler, H., Sekutowicz, M., Brandl, E. J., Müller, D. J., Petrovic, P., & Sterzer, P. (2015). Linking unfounded beliefs to genetic dopamine availability. *Frontiers in Human Neuroscience*, 9, 521. https://doi.org/10.3389/fnhum.2015.00521

Schmolck, H., Buffalo, E. A., Squire, & L. R. (2000). Memory distortions develop over time: Recollections of the O.J. Simpson trial verdict after 15 and 32 months. *Psychological Science*, 11(1), 39–45. https://doi.org/10.1111/1467-9280.00212

Schneiderman, I., Zagoory-Sharon, O., Leckman, J. F., & Feldman, R. (2012). Oxytocin during the initial stages of romantic attachment: Relations to couples' interactive reciprocity. *Psychoneuroendocrinology*, 37(8), 1277–1285. https://doi.org/10.1016/j.psyneuen.2011.12.021

Schrank, W. (1968). The labeling effect of ability grouping. *Journal of Educational Research*, 62(2), 51–52.

Schwind, C., & Buder, J. (2012). Reducing confirmation bias and evaluation bias: When are preference-inconsistent recommendations effective— and when not? *Computers in Human Behavior*, 28(6), 2280–2290. https://doi.org/10.1016/j.chb.2012.06.035

Schyns, P. G., Petro, L. S., & Smith, M. L. (2009). Transmission of facial expressions of emotion co-evolved with their efficient decoding in the brain: Behavioral and brain evidence. *PloS One*, 4(5), e5625. https://doi.org/10.1371/journal.pone.0005625

Scott, G. G., O'Donnell, P. J., & Sereno, S. C. (2012). Emotion words affect eye fixations during reading. Journal of experimental psychology. *Learning, Memory, and Cognition*, 38(3), 783–792. https://doi.org/10.1037/a0027209

Sheng, J. A., Bales, N. J., Myers, S. A., Bautista, A. I., Roueinfar, M., Hale, T. M., & Handa, R. J. (2021). The hypothalamic-pituitary-adrenal axis: Development, programming actions of hormones, and maternal-fetal interactions. *Frontiers in Behavioral Neuroscience*, 14, Article 601939. https://doi.org/10.3389/fnbeh.2020.601939

Sherman, L. E., Michikyan, M., & Greenfield, P. M. (2013). The effects of text, audio, video, and in-person communication on bonding between friends. *Cyberpsychology: Journal of Psychosocial Research on Cyberspace*, 7(2), Article 3. https://doi.org/10.5817/CP2013-2-3

Shi, Y., & Zhu, M. (2023). "Model minorities" in the classroom? Positive evaluation bias towards Asian students and its consequences. *Journal of Public Economics*, 220, Article 104838. https://doi.org/10.1016/j.jpubeco.2023.104838

Shonkoff, J. P., Garner, A. S., Committee on Psychosocial Aspects of Child and Family Health, Committee on Early Childhood, Adoption, and Dependent Care, & Section on Developmental and Behavioral Pediatrics. (2012). The lifelong effects of early childhood adversity and toxic stress. *Pediatrics*, 129(1), e232–e246. https://doi.org/10.1542/peds.2011-2663

Skiba, R. J., Horner, R. H., Chung, C.-G., Rausch, M. K., May, S. L., & Tobin, T. (2011). Race is not neutral: A national investigation of African American and Latino disproportionality in school discipline. *School Psychology Review, 40*(1), 85–107.

Skinner, A. L., & Meltzoff, A. N. (2019). Childhood experiences and intergroup biases among children. *Social Issues and Policy Review, 13*(1), 211–240. https://doi.org/10.1111/sipr.12054

Skowronski, J. J., Betz, A. L., Thompson, C. P., & Shannon, L. (1991). Social memory in everyday life: Recall of self-events and other-events. *Journal of Personality and Social Psychology, 60*(6), 831–843. https://doi.org/10.1037/0022-3514.60.6.831

Skowronski, J. J., & Carlston, D. E. (1987). Social judgment and social memory: The role of cue diagnosticity in negativity, positivity, and extremity biases. *Journal of Personality and Social Psychology, 52*(4), 689–699. https://doi.org/10.1037/0022-3514.52.4.689

Smith, F. W., & Rossit, S. (2018). Identifying and detecting facial expressions of emotion in peripheral vision. *PloS One, 13*(5), Article e0197160. https://doi.org/10.1371/journal.pone.0197160

Sorce, J. F., Emde, R. N., Campos, J. J., & Klinnert, M. D. (1985). Maternal emotional signaling: Its effects on the visual cliff behavior of 1-year-olds. *Developmental Psychology, 21*(1), 195–200. https://doi.org/10.1037/0012-1649.21.1.195

Spreckelmeyer, K. N., Kutas, M., Urbach, T., Altenmüller, E., & Münte, T. F. (2009). Neural processing of vocal emotion and identity. *Brain and Cognition, 69*(1), 121–126. https://doi.org/10.1016/j.bandc.2008.06.003

Stanley, D. A., Sokol-Hessner, P., Fareri, D. S., Perino, M. T., Delgado, M. R., Banaji, M. R., & Phelps, E. A. (2012). Race and reputation: Perceived racial group trustworthiness influences the neural correlates of trust decisions. Philosophical transactions of the Royal Society of London. Series B, *Biological Sciences, 367*(1589), 744–753. https://doi.org/10.1098/rstb.2011.0300

Stark, E. A., Cabral, J., Riem, M. M. E., Van IJzendoorn, M. H., Stein, A., & Kringelbach, M. L. (2020). The power of smiling: The adult brain networks underlying learned infant emotionality. *Cerebral Cortex, 30*(4), 2019–2029. https://doi.org/10.1093/cercor/bhz219

Steele, H., Steele, M., & Croft, C. (2008). Early attachment predicts emotion recognition at 6 and 11 years old. *Attachment & Human Development, 10*(4), 379–393. https://doi.org/10.1080/14616730802461409

Sui, J., Liu, C. H., & Han, S. (2009). Cultural difference in neural mechanisms of self-recognition. *Social Neuroscience, 4*(5), 402–411.

Sun, Y., Ming, L., Sun, J., Guo, F., Li, Q., & Hu, X. (2023). Brain mechanism of unfamiliar and familiar voice processing: An activation likelihood estimation meta-analysis. *PeerJ, 11*, Article e14976. https://doi.org/10.7717/peerj.14976

Sunstein, C. (2002). The law of group polarization. *Journal of Political Philosophy*, *10*(2), 175–195.

Suomi, S. J., Keating, D. P., & Hertzman, C. (Eds.). (1999). *Developmental health and the wealth of nations: Social, biological, and educational dynamics*. Guilford Press.

Talluri, B. C., Urai, A. E., Tsetsos, K., Usher, M., & Donner, T. H. (2018). Confirmation Bias through Selective Overweighting of Choice-Consistent Evidence. *Current Biology*, *28*(19), 3128–3135.e8. https://doi.org/10.1016/j.cub.2018.07.052

Tamietto, M., & de Gelder, B. (2010). Neural bases of the non-conscious perception of emotional signals. *Nature Reviews Neuroscience*, *11*(10), 697–709. https://doi.org/10.1038/nrn2889

Taylor, S. E. (1991). Asymmetrical effects of positive and negative events: The mobilization-minimization hypothesis. *Psychological Bulletin*, *110*(1), 67–85. https://doi.org/10.1037/0033-2909.110.1.67

Ten Velden, F. S., Daughters, K., & De Dreu, C. K. W. (2017). Oxytocin promotes intuitive rather than deliberated cooperation with the in-group. *Hormones and Behavior*, *92*, 164–171. https://doi.org/10.1016/j.yhbeh.2016.06.005

Todd, A. R., Simpson, A. J., Thiem, K. C., & Neel, R. (2016). The generalization of implicit racial bias to young Black boys: Automatic stereotyping or automatic prejudice? *Social Cognition*, *34*(4), 306–323. https://doi.org/10.1521/soco.2016.34.4.306

Todd, A. R., Thiem, K. C., & Neel, R. (2016). Does seeing faces of young Black boys facilitate the identification of threatening stimuli? *Psychological Science*, *27*(3), 384–393. https://doi.org/10.1177/0956797615624492

Treal, T., Jackson, P. L., Jeuvrey, J., Vignais, N., & Meugnot, A. (2021). Natural human postural oscillations enhance the empathic response to a facial pain expression in a virtual character. *Scientific Reports*, *11*(1), 1–10. https://doi.org/10.1038/s41598-021-91710-5

Triandis, H. C. (2018). *Individualism and collectivism*. Routledge.

Umansky, I. M. (2016). To be or not to be EL: An examination of the impact of classifying students as English learners. *Educational Evaluation and Policy Analysis*, *38*(4), 714–737. https://doi.org/10.3102/0162373716664802

Uomini, N. T., & Meyer, G. F. (2013). Shared brain lateralization patterns in language and acheulean stone tool production: A functional transcranial Doppler ultrasound study. *PLoS ONE*, *8*. https://doi.org/10.1371/journal.pone.0072693

U.S. Department of Education, Office for Civil Rights. (2016). *2013–2014 civil rights data collection: A first look*. https://civilrightsdata.ed.gov/assets/downloads/2013-14-first-look.pdf

Vaish, A., & Striano, T. (2004). Is visual reference necessary? Contributions of facial versus vocal cues in 12-month-olds' social

referencing behavior. *Developmental Science*, 7(3), 261–269. https://
doi.org/10.1111/j.1467-7687.2004.00344.x

van der Kooij, K., In 't Veld, L., & Hennink, T. (2021). Motivation as
a function of success frequency. *Motivation and Emotion*, 45(6),
759–768. https://doi.org/10.1007/s11031-021-09904-3

Van Dijk, W. W. (2009). How do you feel? Affective forecasting and the
impact bias in track athletics. *The Journal of Social Psychology*, 149(3),
343–348. https://doi.org/10.3200/SOCP.149.3.343-348

Vaneechoutte, M., & Skoyles, J. R. (1998). The memetic origin of language:
Humans as musical primates. *Journal of Memetics: Evolutionary
Models of Information Transmission*, 2, 84–117. http://users.ugent
.be/~mvaneech/ORILA.FIN.html

Wallman, J. (1992). *Aping language*. Cambridge University Press.

Westen, D., Blagov, P. S., Harenski, K., Kilts, C., & Hamann, S. (2006).
Neural bases of motivated reasoning: An fMRI study of emotional
constraints on partisan political judgment in the 2004 U.S. presiden-
tial election. *Journal of Cognitive Neuroscience*, 18(11), 1947–1958.
https://doi.org/10.1162/jocn.2006.18.11.1947

Whitford, T. J., Jack, B. N., Pearson, D., Griffiths, O., Luque, D., Harris,
A. W. F., Spencer, K. M., & Le Pelley, M. E. (2017). Neurophysiological
evidence of efference copies to inner speech. *eLife*, 6, Article e28197.
https://elifesciences.org/articles/28197

Wickens, J. R., Horvitz, J. C., Costa, R. M., & Killcross, S. (2007). Dopaminergic
mechanisms in actions and habits. *The Journal of Neuroscience: The
Official Journal of the Society for Neuroscience*, 27(31), 8181–8183.
https://doi.org/10.1523/JNEUROSCI.1671-07.2007

Wilson, C. (2014, February 4). Brain zapping makes role of mirror neurons clearer. *New Scientist*. https://www.newscientist.com/article/
dn25002-brain-zapping-makes-role-of-mirror-neurons-clearer/.

Wilson, T. D., & Gilbert, D. T. (2005). Affective forecasting. *Current
Directions in Psychological Science*, 14(3), 131–134. https://doi
.org/10.1111/j.0963-7214.2005.00355.x

Wisse, B., & Sleebos, E. (2016). When change causes stress: Effects of
Self-construal and change consequences. *Journal of Business and
Psychology*, 31, 249–264. https://doi.org/10.1007/s10869-015-9411-z

Wojciszke, B., Baryla, W., Szymków-Sudziarska, A., Parzuchowski, M., &
Kowalczyk, K. (2009). Saying is experiencing: Affective consequences
of complaining and affirmation. *Polish Psychological Bulletin*, 40(2),
74–84. https://journals.pan.pl/Content/107612/PDF/38.pdf

Wolfe, J. M., & Utochkin, I. S. (2019). What is a preattentive feature?
Current Opinion in Psychology, 29, 19–26. https://doi.org/10.1016/j
.copsyc.2018.11.005

Wood, A., Rychlowska, M., Korb, S., Niedenthal, P. (2016). Fashioning
the face: sensorimotor simulation contributes to facial expression

recognition. *Trends in Cognitive Sciences, 20*(3), 227–240. https://doi
.org/10.1016/j.tics.2015.12.010

Woodzicka, J. A., & LaFrance, M. (2001). Real versus imagined gender harassment. *Journal of Social Issues, 57*(1), 15-30. https://doi
.org/10.1111/0022-4537.00199

Xiao, N. G., Quinn, P. C., Liu, S., Ge, L., Pascalis, O., & Lee, K. (2018). Older but not younger infants associate own-race faces with happy music and other-race faces with sad music. *Developmental Science, 21*(2), 10.1111/desc.12537. https://doi.org/10.1111/desc.12537

Xiao, N. G., Wu, R., Quinn, P. C., Liu, S., Tummeltshammer, K. S., Kirkham, N. Z., Ge, L., Pascalis, O., & Lee, K. (2018). Infants Rely More on Gaze Cues From Own-Race Than Other-Race Adults for Learning Under Uncertainty. Child development, 89(3), e229–e244. https://doi
.org/10.1111/cdev.12798

Xue, C., Calapai, A., Krumbiegel, J., & Treue, S. (2020). Sustained spatial attention accounts for the direction bias of human microsaccades. *Scientific Reports, 10*(1), Article 20604. https://doi.org/10.1038/
s41598-020-77455-7

Yuan, J., Ju, E., Meng, X., Chen, X., Zhu, S., Yang, J., & Li, H. (2015). Enhanced brain susceptibility to negative stimuli in adolescents: ERP evidences. *Frontiers in Behavioral Neuroscience, 9*, 98. https://doi
.org/10.3389/fnbeh.2015.00098

Zhou, J. (2012). The effects of reciprocal imitation on teacher–student relationships and student learning outcomes. *Mind, Brain, and Education, 6*(2), 66–73. https://doi.org/10.1111/j.1751-228X.2012.01140.x

Zhu, Y., Zhang, L., Fan, J., & Han, S. (2007). Neural basis of cultural influence on self-representation. *Neuroimage, 34*(3), 1310–1316. https://
doi.org/10.1016/j.neuroimage.2006.08.047

INDEX

A Sage Company

CORWIN HAS ONE MISSION: to enhance education through intentional professional learning.

We build long-term relationships with our authors, educators, clients, and associations who partner with us to develop and continuously improve the best evidence-based practices that establish and support lifelong learning.

Solutions
YOU WANT

Experts
YOU TRUST

Results
YOU NEED

INSTITUTES

Corwin Institutes provide regional and virtual events where educators collaborate with peers and learn from industry experts. Prepare to be recharged and motivated!

corwin.com/institutes

ON-SITE PROFESSIONAL LEARNING

Corwin on-site PD is delivered through high-energy keynotes, practical workshops, and custom coaching services designed to support knowledge development and implementation.

www.corwin.com/pd

VIRTUAL PROFESSIONAL LEARNING

Our virtual PD combines live expert facilitation with the flexibility of anytime, anywhere professional learning. See the power of intentionally designed virtual PD.

www.corwin.com/virtualworkshops

CORWIN ONLINE

Online learning designed to engage, inform, challenge, and inspire. Our courses offer practical, classroom-focused instruction that will meet your continuing education needs and enhance your practice.

www.corwinonline.com

PLSN209A8

Visit **www.corwin.com**